Joe's
Allotment

Joe's
Allotment

Planning and planting a productive plot

Joe Swift

**Foreword by
Toby Buckland**

This book is published to accompany the television series entitled
Gardeners' World.

10 9 8 7 6 5 4 3 2 1

Published in 2009 by BBC Books, an imprint of Ebury Publishing.
A Random House Group Company

The Random House Group Limited Reg. No. 954009

Addresses for companies within the Random House Group can be found
at **www.randomhouse.co.uk**

A CIP catalogue record for this book is available from the British Library.

ISBN 978 1 84 607672 5

The Random House Group Limited supports The Forest Stewardship Council
(FSC), the leading international forest certification organization. All our titles
that are printed on Greenpeace approved FSC certified paper carry the FSC logo.
Our paper procurement policy can be found at **www.rbooks.co.uk/environment**

Commissioning editor: Lorna Russell
Project editor: Caroline McArthur
Copy editor: Helena Caldon
Designer: Smith & Gilmour
Production controller: Bridget Fish

All photography by Sarah Cuttle except for the following:
pp. 19, 37, 47, 67 (1–4), 92–3, 171 (1) © Mark Scott; pp. 32, 36, 45 © Joe Swift;
p. 39 (1) © David Askham/Garden Picture Library; (2) © Jacqui Hurst/Garden
Picture Library; (3) © Maddie Thornhill/GAP Photos, (4) © Michael Howes/GAP
Photos, (6) © Howard Rice/Garden Picture Library; (8) Paul Debois/GAP Photos;
(9) © Ron Sutherland/Garden Picture Library; p. 64 © Joy Larkcom; p. 77 (1)
© Clive Nichols/GAP Photos; 118 © Alamy; pp. 140, 206 © BBC Worldwide;
p. 182 © Siobhan O'Donohghue

Colour origination by: Altaimage
Printed and bound in Italy by Printer Trento

Mixed Sources
Product group from well-managed
forests and other controlled sources
www.fsc.org   Cert no. CQ-COC-000012
© 1996 Forest Stewardship Council
FSC

Contents

Foreword

It's never easy taking on a new allotment, what with the weeds, the high hopes and the pressure of being watched by sceptical allotment neighbours. I well remember taking on my first plot and the particularly officious allotment secretary who told me in no uncertain terms that the committee wouldn't be pleased if I brought black bean aphid onto the plots. As if I was intending to smuggle them in for fun!

So pity poor Joe who had the nation's gardeners to impress too. I'll admit, when Joe's plot first appeared on our screens I wondered if he'd bitten off more than he could chew. But when I visited him in the summer I couldn't have been more impressed. There were raised beds fashioned from salvaged timber and brimming with produce; compost heaps working their alchemy; even a shed to keep his seeds and tools dry – and knowing Joe, possibly a radio tuned to Arsenal FM and a couple of beers. It was a brilliant success.

I've been an allotmenteer for nigh on ten years and well know the pleasures of picking and eating home-grown food. It has more flavour, is quicker to cook – you can taste its vitality – but just as important is the rhythm of planting and harvesting. The magic of an allotment is that it turns conventional food values on their head – and vegetables considered mundane when bought from the supermarket become precious and worthy of celebration. When Joe cooked up that first new potato from his plot I knew the pleasure he'd got from growing it, and the delight of picking each fresh strawberry-heart, every pea-pod and pumpkin. It's these small victories that inspire gardeners to get out and plant more.

This book captures all of that and also the spirit of freedom and self-expression provided by allotments. Where else can you experiment with stuff salvaged from skips without offending the neighbours? Where else can you make do and mend with such oblivious flair? Allotments stand apart as bastions of liberty where the value of time and being close to the soil can truly be felt.

Joe's efforts, broadcast every Friday evening on BBC *Gardeners' World* and in the pages of this book, are a great triumph, showing clearly how to grow and harvest crops. But perhaps the real achievement is that his hard work and enthusiasm have gathered in a whole new generation of gardeners as they sow, hoe and plant and make their world a better place.

Toby Buckland

Introduction

To say 'I've always wanted an allotment and to grow my own' simply wouldn't be telling the truth. My gardening interests and career have always been connected to the more ornamental elements of garden design: landscaping, planting, and generally beautifying gardens to create inviting, practical and visually successful spaces.

Until recently, the thought of growing fruit and veg simply didn't enter my head. This may also have something to do with my parents, as they have never grown vegetables (although I have finally forgiven them!), so when I was a child we weren't aware of the seasonal processes nor did we have the physical contact of produce freshly dug from the soil. In my mind our small London garden was a place solely to play football. In fact, when I was a kid I was actually one of those fussy eaters who avoided most vegetables on my plate. (This seems rather ironic, as in my twenties I became a devout pescatarian, and even now I only eat fish and fowl and love vegetables – well, apart from a couple!)

Over the last few years my views on growing fruit and vegetables have completely changed, and I'm hooked! I genuinely love it. I now get more excited about going to the allotment than into my back garden, and sometimes look at a wonderful ornamental planting combination and say to myself, 'well, it looks great, but you can't eat it'.

For many years Monty, Carol, Toby and Alys were in control of the vegetable garden at Berryfields for *Gardeners' World*. It was their domain, and I felt very out of place in it, thinking for some crazy reason that there was a mystique and hidden secret to growing your own. A couple of years ago they all encouraged me to have a go in the container vegetable garden at Berryfields, planting up pots, recycled olive-oil tins and some old tyres with a range of produce. Although I had a few failures, on the whole everything grew extremely well and I was quite staggered at the results. For such a tiny space, I actually got a pretty good crop in the first year.

Lifting potatoes, carrots and a few salad leaves and eating them as fresh as they would ever be was a magic moment. It was right there and then that I understood the satisfaction of doing it, and why the others were so evangelical about it. It's absolutely true that there is nothing like eating food that you've grown yourself; it simply tastes better than anything you can buy.

Carrots have never been my favourite vegetable, but my first crop of them tasted so sweet – very different from any shop bought ones – and I now can't get enough of them.

Growing for the family

At this time our family was eating organic produce courtesy of an organic box that was delivered on a weekly basis. It was a great service, but I did have some issues with it. For a start, you get what you're given each week – which is basically whatever's in season locally – plus a few carefully selected imports. The produce was definitely good quality, but you certainly pay for the service of selection and delivery. Our local farmers' market also has some good produce, but, again, it is a really expensive way to stock up on your staples. Our other source of food is, of course, supermarkets. Even though we, like most other people, use them, they do wind me up something rotten. They seem to buy in their produce for regularity of shape and size, rather than considering the all-important flavour, let alone the air miles involved in producing and importing them. Then there's the excessive packaging: needless plastic bags all over the house once you've unpacked.

The thought of being able to bypass these issues by growing my own organic, environmentally sound food, together with my fledgling attempts and success at Berryfields, gave me the desire and confidence I needed to spur me on. I knew that the only way to really learn how to do it was to have a go.

Our small, urban family garden has had the designer treatment, and although we use it all the time it's not somewhere I could grow crops, so taking on an allotment seemed the best idea. I only have to look around my friends and family to see encouragement on all sides. My ultra-keen, gardening mother-in-law, Brenda, has an allotment in Cambridge, and my children love to go and visit her and help her plant and harvest. Many other friends of mine also have plots and rave about them, including my good friend and garden designer, Cleve West, who has a fabulous allotment near Hampton Court, which he simply couldn't live without, and which he practically lives on during his spare time over the summer months.

Aged eleven and nine now, the kids are growing up fast, and I am aware that soon they'll be teenagers and find the allotment thing 'just so boooooring dad', which was another factor in thinking that now was the ideal time for us to do this as a family. Taking on an allotment gave the kids somewhere where they could have an area to themselves to grow anything they wanted and have a really good dig. Gardening is one of the healthiest exercises around, and I believe that it's great to get children started on it early on, as it's a skill they'll have for life.

Of course, there's also the matter of the all-important healthy food that

The allotment teaches my kids where food comes from in an informal, engaging and fun way. I know they'll never lose the skills they've picked up, and I hope one day they'll go on to grow their own. Who knows, they might even take on allotments of their own.

we grow. Like many parents I want my children to benefit from good food produced without chemicals or any messing about. Although they are healthy eaters anyway, the children eat, and especially enjoy, our crops because they've helped to grow them themselves and are excited by the whole process. To be honest, the allotment has also proved to be a really cheap way of entertaining them for hours on end, as the whole plot costs £77 for the year (it would be half that if I were a resident of the borough). That's about the same for all of us to go to the cinema and get a bowl of noodles on the way home – once. Not bad, eh?

The support of my family in this gardening adventure has been a real bonus; they wanted to get involved too, so ultimately it was a unanimous decision to take on the allotment. Time had to be a major consideration, or lack of it. During the busiest gardening times of the year I'm usually crazily zooming around filming as well as helping to run a garden-design business. It all comes at once in my industry, and I knew an allotment wouldn't exactly look after itself. Fortunately, by taking on an allotment for *Gardeners' World*, it was agreed that some of my filming time could be taken up there, which helped, but still I knew it would take up plenty more of my own time and be a big commitment to make it work and keep on top of it.

Gardening in the community

I soon found out that as well as being productive spaces, most allotments have a wonderful sense of community. The combined knowledge of the other allotmenteers is phenomenal, and in an urban setting there will always be an interesting mix of backgrounds, cultures, and ages. There are the die-hard allotmenteers who have been doing it for years and have seen many 'youngsters' and 'yuppies' like myself come and go. In our defence (and the fleeting allotment owners aside), it is exciting to see the revival of allotments in our hectic, technology-driven, modern-day world, and it lifts the spirits to see a new generation of younger people and families who want to reconnect with nature, enjoy the process of growing and understand where their food comes from. Some of these people may have had gardening experience in the past, but many live in flats and for them the allotment is their only outside space.

On my site many of the gardeners are retired and see tending their allotment as a full-time job – often spending up to four hours a day doing it. If only… Although allotments undoubtedly need time and attention,

1 Keith runs me through his latest device. **2** Vincenzo may be in his late 80s, but working on the plot keeps him looking great. **3** If Manuel could grow his own tobacco, he surely would. **4** Ken in his standard pose – leaning on his spade!

and that kind of care is the ideal, I do also think that even those of us with less time to spare can still make an impact on a plot. And, happily, rather than dismissing my more part-time efforts, the die-harders are pleased to see newcomers get the bug, and I've found they are always only too willing to offer help and advice from their experience and wisdom.

This book takes a look back at my first year on the plot and all the successes, failures, triumphs and mishaps I experienced along the way. To say this time on my allotment has been a huge learning curve would be an understatement. Looking back on my early, enthusiastic days, I had overcooked, possibly crazy, and unrealistic ambitions for my first year. I wanted to get the whole 250-square-metre plot organized, in shape, and producing enough to replace the veggie box delivery.

Having said that, I have come a long way. The main structure is in, the weeds are fewer than when I took it on, and my soil has greatly improved due to all the work we put in at the start. Sure, there have been times when it was all getting on top of me and I felt I couldn't cope and almost chucked it all in – going away for a couple of weeks and coming back to a sea of weeds, or losing every single tomato to blight can be absolutely soul destroying. In all, though, it has been a fabulous, deeply satisfying and worthwhile experience. I've learnt a huge amount, made some good friends and produced plenty of food so far. I say so far because I know that, as in all forms of gardening, things never finish, they just roll on.

···⟩
Ken and I hit it off from the first day we met. He adores his allotment but gives away most of his veg to friends and family. My wife Cathy turned that parsnip into one of the best soups ever.

Before anything else

Once I had made the decision to take on an allotment there was no turning back. I had my mind set on the idea that I would soon be living the good life. I hadn't even contemplated the issue of finding a local plot, as I naively thought it would be a case of phoning up the local council, picking my favourite location, signing on the dotted line and paying my rent.

How wrong could I be? Most of London seemed to have the same desire. Hackney is my local borough, and when I started to make enquiries I found that there were only nine allotment sites in the area, which had a total of 124 plots between them. So, not surprisingly, with around 210,000 residents in the borough, not one of the plots was available. A rough calculation reveals the sad fact that there is one plot for approximately 1,700 people! Shocking. In fact, at that time there was a long waiting list with the guesstimate being that it would be a minimum of three years before a plot would become available; but now even the waiting list has been officially closed as there are far too many names on it already. Put quite simply – allotments are bloody gold dust round here.

So, slightly disheartened but not put off, I widened my search further towards Islington, Haringey and Camden; but I still had no joy as all of those were fully booked and also had long waiting lists. (Islington's being a terrifying ten years. Too long to wait.) I was discovering that the bigger issue with all inner-city areas is that population is high and as a result, space is seriously squeezed. Therefore, land being expensive and in huge demand, many allotment sites, along with school playing fields and suchlike, have been sold off for housing developments.

I do hope that the renewed interest in growing your own means that these spaces are valued and fully protected in the future. Haven't we learnt anything from our mistakes? Rather than building on allotment sites to create new homes with little or no outside space and suffering all the social and environmental issues that go with them, why don't developers and planners look at sustainable solutions for integrating growing and green space? Okay, I can see that the traditional allotment as we know it may not be the solution to these new spaces, which is a shame, but surely there's a way to make it work with some clever planning and good design.

I want a plot

I was becoming impatient. I just wanted to get on with it, and get stuck in preparing the soil for the year ahead so I could begin to produce some food; after all, that was what it was all about. But instead I was caught up with websites and being put 'on hold' on the phone for hours on end and, as yet, still no joy. Now I was becoming disheartened, and I felt as if it just wasn't going to happen. My vision had been that the allotment would be just around the corner or on the way to the kids' school so I could pop in and out whilst dropping them off or picking them up. In my mind we'd spend long summer evenings after work and at the weekends sitting in a secluded, tranquil spot eating fresh salads with a glass of wine in hand before ambling the short walk home to bed.

In reality, though, wherever my idyll was it certainly wasn't going to be close enough to walk to, so I had to spread my search even further afield – into the suburbs of Redbridge and Enfield. The odds looked better here as Enfield has 37 allotment sites which cover 76 hectares and provide around 3,000 plots. Now that's more like it. Fortunately, the council had plenty of sites that were immediately available, so I arranged to meet the allotment officer to show me around a few. Enfield has a strong heritage of gardening and horticulture, with plenty of nurseries and garden centres (many of which I knew well), so I thought it would be good to be a part of it. It was an eye-opening afternoon.

There are some huge sites, some that I had seen whilst driving up and down the busy A10 dual carriageway. The first I was taken to was one of these very sites, and there I was shown a selection of interesting and varied allotments. One I remember distinctly had a 'shanty town' sort of structure on it, complete with covered seating area and shed. It was quite bizarre. The soil was pretty good, but it had an issue in common with many of the other plots: it was too close to the busy road. Although I met some fabulous characters that day, I couldn't escape the sound of the traffic on the sites adjacent to the main road. Having lived in London my entire life I was adamant that if I was to spend hours and hours on a plot I wanted to have at least the feeling of escaping the city, which, for me, is impossible if I can hear the constant rumble of articulated lorries.

After chatting to the allotment officer about this issue, he took us to a couple of other, quieter, sites. One was extremely tidy with a lovely, well-kept, weed-free plot. I was seriously tempted, but it was shoehorned in amongst the other plots and I just felt that it might end up being like gardening in a goldfish bowl. It may sound silly, but remember I'm 'that gardener chap on the telly', too, and it's nice to be able to get on with it without feeling as if you're being watched – even if you aren't really. The last plot I saw was the one that I immediately felt was right for us – and the one that, ultimately, I went for. What caught my imagination about it was that it was on a very open, quiet site that had a real feeling of space. It seemed to have a rural element to it, and it also backed onto a park with football pitches. Perfect. If the kids got bored they could go there and have a kick-about, and if I got bored I could watch a game of footy!

On this site there were quite a few plots available. It was a very cold November day and there weren't many allotmenteers around, except for one chap, Keith, who was approachable and had a really good-looking plot. It was obvious that he knew what he was doing. The full-sized plot right next to him was available, and although it had lots of weeds on it at the time, I could see from Keith's plot that the soil was actually pretty good quality. I had a little test dig and, sure enough, although the soil was clay based and compacted it was actually okay and looked like it had been cultivated in the distant past.

A proud moment as a new allotment holder finds his very own plot. 'How handy', I thought at the time, 'the water supply is right next to it.' Looking back I should have asked myself why no one else had snapped it up!

Part of the deal with Enfield council is that they scrape the plot free of all the top growth, so the weeds, which I thought at that time consisted of mainly grasses and a few brambles, didn't worry me too much. The site had lockers, toilets and a parking area, and Keith had also organised huge deliveries of free compost made from the local boroughs' green waste. There were mounds of this rich, dark compost on most plots, as if an enormous mole had been through the site. My intended plot also had a water tank sitting right next to it, so all in all it seemed to be a real result. I suppose I should have known something was up. No one told me about the horsetail!

Choosing an allotment

Most allotments are council-owned, so your first call should be to your local council, or you can check out their website. These allotments may be statutory, which means they are protected by law, or possibly temporary sites on leased or rented land where long-term tenancy is not agreed. There are some privately-owned allotments, too, and the best way to find out about availability is to ask a plot holder.

Allotment sizes

Allotments are measured in rods, perches or poles (the same thing, just different terminology) one of which is the equivalent to around 5 metres, or 5 1/2 yards. The dimensions of a 10-rod allotment are 10 x 5m/5.5yards x 5m/5.5yards, which equals 253 sq meters or 302.5 sq yards. Most plots are around 10 rods, but many are offered as half, quarter, or even smaller sized plots. Mine is a full-sized 10-rod plot.

What to look for when choosing a plot

Although I love my plot and wouldn't change it, knowing what I know now I would have other criteria if I were choosing a plot again. When you visit a plot for the first time, there are certain things you should look out for:

🌿 Talk to others and look at their plots

Talk to some of the other allotment holders and find out as much about the site as possible. Is there an on-site committee? How are things organized? How are the other plots and their plants looking? Are they thriving or struggling, and are they well kept or smothered in pernicious weeds (which could give you real problems)?

🌿 Check the soil

If the plot is covered in weeds, remove some to expose a little soil and dig in to examine its character. From this, consider what and how much soil improving needs to be done.

🌿 Look at the lie of the land

If the plot is on a slope, different areas will retain water to differing degrees: the lower areas may be prone to waterlogging whereas the higher ground may dry out quickly. The lower areas may also create a frost pocket, which will affect what you choose to grow there.

🌿 Assess the shade

Sunlight and shade have an important influence on crops, and although some light shade is useful in certain areas (to protect sensitive crops in summer and provide shade for a possible seating area, for example) a heavily shaded plot will seriously restrict what you can grow.

🌿 Make a note of the existing paths and structures

Some plots will have been abandoned with some infrastructure left in place. Assess the routes and quality of any pathways and consider whether they could be left in place in the short or long term, or whether they could be adapted to suit your own proposed layout. If there isn't one there already, most allotment sites will allow you to erect a shed, and I have found mine extremely useful for keeping seeds dry, chitting potatoes, storing tools, potting up and having the odd cuppa! Like most men, I love a shed. You will probably need to apply in writing to your council for permission, but some sites supply sheds with plots or you may choose a plot with a shed already in situ.

🌿 Check the access

Access is important. On my plot I am relatively close to where the council compost gets delivered, which is extremely handy, whereas others have a long barrow run to their plots. I'm not too far from the toilets and lockers either. On the other hand, the plots further away from the amenities are a little more private and have more a sense of seclusion.

Look for weeds
If you have weeds on your plot, determine what they are and how bad the problem is. If you are looking during the winter months, have a dig around for perennial weeds such as couch grass or horsetail.

Find out about facilities and parking
We have toilets, secure lockers and some parking on our site, which are all extremely useful. Not all allotments provide these, whereas others go further and have a shop with seeds, plants and tools – and some I've seen even have an organized café!

Check on security
Provision of site security is often included within a tenancy agreement. If vandals are intent on entering the site there's often little that can be done, but secure fences and gates will certainly deter them.

Ask about communal days
Is there a notice board with arranged activities? This is a sign of an organized and friendly site. Of course, you can choose whether to get involved or not.

Work out travelling time
Think carefully about how you'll get to and from your plot, and how long it'll take. In an ideal world we all want a site just around the corner, but be realistic, as in most places it's unlikely with the demand. If it's too far to walk, look into the local transport links.

Knowing what you take on

The most important thing to consider when taking on an allotment is, is it actually going to work for you, or will it become something else you struggle to keep up with in your very busy life? An allotment needs some degree of commitment, so there are a few things you should consider before signing on the dotted line.

Time
A single weekly visit is about the minimum amount of time you'll need to spend maintaining your allotment, although it's easy to spend way more time there than that, especially when initially setting up and also at key periods of the year – such as watering in hot, dry spells and when harvesting.

Physical capabilities
Gardening is fabulous exercise. However, do consider your own level of fitness before taking on a large plot. Some soils can be hard work, and if you aren't used to regular exercise, take it at your own pace and work within your limits. Over time you'll build up strength and dexterity and you should find it easier.

Costs
If you're starting from scratch and you don't already own a garden, the most expensive part of starting an allotment is probably buying the tools (see page 202). You may then want to move on to installing a shed, fruit cage, raised beds, and even a greenhouse, which of course can all add up. The rent of the plot and any travel costs should also be considered.

Legal aspects of owning a plot

On paper there is nothing more simple than asking your council for an allotment, paying the rent, collecting the key and getting cracking. But that key usually comes with a leaflet of rules and regulations. You must do this, you mustn't do that, and for heaven's sake never do the other on your plot…

SITE RULES

Seriously though, the rules come from the management committee of your site. My plot is managed directly by the council, so they have drawn up the rules; other sites are managed by a committee based at the site and usually the same rules apply – with perhaps a few additional ones. Basically these boil down to you having to keep your plot well tended (you can't let weeds overrun the place), clearly marking the boundaries of your plot, and there's usually something about their policies on greenhouses, sheds and livestock.

On our site no one had a shed but I wanted one. The main reason was that I wanted to shelter when it rained (the locker room and car park aren't that cosy) and the camera crew needed somewhere to put cameras in heavy rain. But the rules and regulations stated that we had to apply for permission to build one. So I did, and the allotment officer said it was fine. The same goes for greenhouses (I might apply) and livestock (Keith applied and got his chickens passed).

We did also have to make an emergency phone call to the council to check out a regulation when we were filming the tomato blight that cruelly struck down everyone's plants on the same night in early September. Blight is nasty and we wanted to film me burning the plants and affected fruit. However, the rules state no bonfires between April and October, with a £2000 fine for anyone breaking this particular rule. And that kind of money is a few years' worth of plot rent. After we assured the council we weren't annoying anyone or causing a nuisance they gave it the okay, and the blight was burnt, the cameras rolled and the nation watched a week later.

On another occasion we had to contact the council to ask if a growing mound of rubbish could be moved. Of course it was in part because we wanted to film my plot and the mound was getting in the back of shot, but it was also beginning to attract vermin. The mound itself was the result of a new regulation that came into force a few weeks after I took on my allotment. All carpet had to be removed from every plot for two reasons: the first was that certain chemicals in the carpets were suspected of leaching

Of course you don't have to limit yourself to growing fruit and veg on your plot; you can grow anything you want. At home my garden isn't big enough to provide cut flowers for the house, but during the summer I always took home a decent bunch with my veggies.

into the soil; the second was that our council provides a free scrape of the plot when it is first signed over and the carpets, the mainstay of many a path on allotments up and down the country, clogs up the machinery. We all fully understood the new regulation and had all stuck by it, and so the carpet mound had appeared. Happily, the council duly came, moved the mound, and everyone was happy.

My main piece of advice to anyone taking on an allotment is to read the rules of the site, abide by them, and ask your management team, council or fellow plot holders for permission to do anything that appears to be outside of the rules. Don't be afraid of talking to your site rep, officer, or whoever gets things done, either, as they're there to work for and with you.

HOW MUCH OWNERSHIP DO YOU HAVE?

Land is at a premium in every city, and it is still highly valued even in more rural areas. There is an ever-increasing demand for new housing and allotment sites are prime targets for these homes – make no mistake. Usually allotment sites are slap bang in the middle of housing estates and act as a green barrier to the ends of two separate estates, so it's no wonder that developers want to get their hands on the land. So, in addition to all the other factors, when looking at your plot check out its status – or who is responsible for the terms on which it is managed.

Here's a quick guide:

🍃 Statutory allotments are on sites that are set aside by councils solely for use as allotments. These sites cannot be sold or used for any other purpose other than allotments without the consent of the Secretary of State for Transport, Local Government and the Regions.

🍃 Temporary allotments are on land that is allocated for other uses but that is leased or rented by an allotment's authority. The problem is that these sites are not protected in the same way as statutory sites. In other words, they are easily sold off to anyone offering the right cash.

🍃 There are some privately-owned sites around the country where land is used for allotments. It should come as no surprise that these sites don't have much protection and private sites are very much like temporary ones, in that the council has no control over them.

The sale of allotment sites does concern me. Okay, I'm new to allotmenteering, but some people have had their plots for years, decades in some cases, and for many it is a very – if not *the* most important – part

of their life. However, if your site has been earmarked for another use, temporary and privately-owned allotments can easily be sold off. Statutory sites, as I've said above, do need that permission from government, and before they say yes to any sale they need to be satisfied that:

- The allotment is either not necessary or is surplus to requirements.
- The council will give displaced plot holders adequate alternative sites, unless this is not necessary or practicable.
- The council has taken the number of people on the waiting list into account when making their decision to sell off sites.
- The council has actively promoted and publicized the availability of allotment sites and has consulted the National Society of Allotment and Leisure Gardeners (NSALG).

This all sounds negative, but be reassured that the government has to communicate with the plot holders before the plots are sold off. If the plots are well tended, with a good uptake, and you, or a site representative, are talking to the council about the situation, they will not be sold off – without one heck of a fight. Hold on to your plot!

On a more positive note, and they will probably hate me for saying this, but after all the doom and gloom of sell offs, aside from the inner London boroughs, which are exempt, councils still have legal obligations to provide allotments. In a perfect world everyone should have access to an allotment at the most a bike ride, but ideally walking, distance from his or her home; but I'm a realist, and in London and other cities there's no chance of this. However, the council is legally obliged to consider all applications for a plot.

Better still, if you want a plot, get five like-minded individuals together and write a letter to your council – they then have to consider developing a new site. They don't have to actually do it, but they have a duty to consider it. I know of people who have gone one step further and identified wasteland, got a group of people together and successfully applied for the use to be changed to an allotment site. They received funding, organized themselves into a self-managed group, and converted the land into a top-class site. Within the year the plots were productive, they had organized a social hut to be delivered and the site now has a waiting list for plots. It's an old saying, but one worth repeating: 'if you don't ask, you don't get'. My apologies now go to every council official who will be bombarded with letters requesting allotments. Actually, no, they don't, as everyone who wants one should have a plot. So, come on councils – make it happen.

Waiting lists

As I mentioned earlier, my nearest allotment site has actually closed its waiting list because the popularity of plots is increasing all the time. One story I heard was that a 30-year waiting list in one area prompted some parents to put the names of their newborn sons and daughters on the local allotment waiting list!

Obviously the first port of call is the council, and then I would advise you to nag away at them. Look around sites and make a note of the number of unkempt plots; because that's the really frustrating thing about allotment sites, there are long waiting list for plots on sites where quite clearly there are plots that haven't seen a spade for years. This is because some councils have muddled records on who rents what: others may be concerned at the possibility of incurring legal costs in trying to move on plot holders who don't dig, but also don't want to leave. I'm not having a go at any particular council, but wouldn't it be great if they all tidied up their records to help meet the increased demand for plots? After all, it's a demand that isn't going to go away in a hurry.

PLOT FACTS:

- There are around 300,000 allotments in the UK.
- 200,000 allotments have been lost since the late 1970s (some would say that's a little careless, so where are they? Oh, under housing no one now wants).
- You can expect to yield around £300-worth of produce every year from a full-sized plot.
- Expect to pay anything between £20 and £150 per year in rent for your plot (mine is £77 including water, but if I lived in the borough it would be cheaper).

In the beginning

The day I picked up my allotment keys was extremely exciting. It felt a little like my first day at school all over again, except there weren't any lessons or any teachers around to tell me what to do. The first time I put some tools into my locker I expected a teacher's hand on my shoulder and to hear a dour voice asking me why I was late for class. Must be the sign of a misspent youth or something, but when I realized that it was now my space to do with whatever I wanted, I felt totally liberated.

Gardening at home had always involved working around space restrictions and trying to make the site work on a practical and aesthetic level, but now I had taken on my very first piece of land solely for the purpose of growing fruit and veg, and it didn't particularly matter what it looked like. As a garden designer I'm used to considering clients' requests and needs, but here I could do as I pleased. From now on it was all about production, learning, and getting out of it what I put in. The plan was to also have plenty of fun and get fit. Some people take gardening far too seriously, in my opinion, and get competitive with it. Surely, growing your own is a personal journey, and I for one like to do things my own way.

In the spirit of this, I wanted to personalize our allotment and very much make it ours, rather than following a standard layout. I didn't really have any thoughts at that time about how to do this, I needed to get some basic materials together first. Of course you don't see many new materials on allotments as they can quickly cost more than the annual rent of the plot, but allotmenteers are also at the forefront of recycling anything and everything they can get their hands on. I started to see things at home that I was thinking of getting rid of in a whole new light and I still have a problem walking past a skip without having a look for anything that could be converted into something useful at the plot!

I tried not to think about it being such a public project, either, as I was aware there might be some real sticklers watching, just waiting for me to trip up. The idea behind using my allotment in the series was to leave me to it in an observational, documentary kind of way: following all the real trials and tribulations of a first-time allotmenteer and showing the reality of someone like myself taking it on. Okay, undoubtedly my 23 years of professional gardening would help, but this was genuinely my first attempt at anything like this.

Getting started

A week or so after I took over my plot the allotment officer came and scraped it with his JCB, which is part of the service for allotment holders in Enfield if the plot is overgrown with weeds. I made sure I was there that day as I wanted to see precisely what I was dealing with and also because I didn't want him to scrape too deeply, thereby removing my precious topsoil.

It was a cold, wet January day, and as he scraped I jumped onto the soil to have a dig around. What I found was pretty much what I was used to, having gardened in London for many years. I had been given a clay-based soil, which is hard work but pretty fertile. However, it was also seriously compacted. (The digger having just driven over it didn't help the cause either.)

Once the digger had left, the plot looked clean and absolutely enormous. Suddenly I was left facing an empty rectangle of mud, with thousands of weed roots hiding just below the surface. Oh Lord, what had I taken on? Keith next door was retired and spent hours every day working his plot, but I was already squeezed for time and it was only January. I felt a little sick as I went home that night.

It's incredible what a digger can do in an hour or two. I wanted to be there to make sure it scraped off the weedy top growth, but left the topsoil in place. It may be a superficial solution as the weeds' roots are left in the ground, but it still saved days' worth of work by hand.

Planning the plot

So, you've got your keys to the site gate, but what happens next? The temptation is that you rush in and try to dig the whole lot over in a weekend, put your back out, then spend the rest of it cursing your initial thought that an allotment was anywhere near a good idea.

Keep the spade in the shed for the moment, the only tool you need at first is a piece of paper.

You're not marking out beds yet, but rather a list of what you want to grow. Vegetables, fruit (and their resultant cages), herbs, cut flowers, plants for wildlife – all could have a place in your allotment, and once written down your mind will start to automatically lay out your plot.

When you're planning your harvest, consider growing vegetables that you can't easily buy – either from a supermarket, farmers' market or box scheme. Then there's the economics of vegetables. Some would argue that it isn't worth growing maincrop potatoes, for example, as they are so cheap, readily available and, to be honest, pretty tasty when bought from shops. Why use up precious space on something you can by for pennies? I did actually think about this when I started, but because potatoes do take up a fair bit of space and my plot looked enormous when I first took it over, I did grow some spuds. How I grew them comes later in this book (see page 84), but I will say that once you have tasted your own spuds, whether earlies or mains, there is no turning back. Having said that, I do think the no-spud plot is a good plan if you have only half a plot.

The same level of consideration goes for other crops. Broad beans, runner beans and French beans all require you to be at the plot and picking at least every week; if you miss a couple of weeks you are in danger of allowing your crops to go over. Onions and garlic, however, all crop at roughly the same time and can be harvested in a day to be stored for a good length of time. So perhaps these are better crops to grow, or at least might be higher up on your wish list.

We sat down as a family and made up our list of what we wanted to grow and eat, which really helped to focus our minds, but was also quite a laugh. Of course my kids, Connie and Stanley, wanted to grow the unachievable oranges and bananas (and baked beans already in their tins!), but in no time we had a good list of what we all liked and what we thought was realistic in our first year.

GETTING IT DOWN ON PAPER

When I first saw it I have to admit that I felt daunted by the sight (courtesy of Enfield council) of my freshly cleared plot. However, once I'd put down on paper the list of crops I wanted to grow, it made it easier for me to decide where they would go.

My design included putting in raised beds and making paths using the free wood chippings supplied by the council and a local tree surgeon. Decent paths are vital on an allotment. You should design any paths so that you can get to all your beds or rows without walking on the soil: you will do so much damage to your soil if you are clambering all over it to get to weed a row of carrots or plant your brassicas.

Access is the watchword, too. Make paths wide enough for you and a wheelbarrow, or, if you have a film crew plodding behind with their tripods, a little bit wider still!

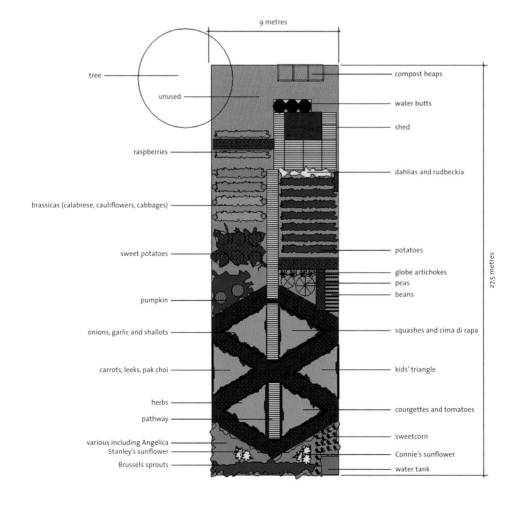

9 metres

27.5 metres

tree
unused
raspberries
brassicas (calabrese, cauliflowers, cabbages)
sweet potatoes
pumpkin
onions, garlic and shallots
carrots, leeks, pak choi
herbs
pathway
various including Angelica
Stanley's sunflower
Brussels sprouts

compost heaps
water butts
shed
dahlias and rudbeckia
potatoes
globe artichokes
peas
beans
squashes and cima di rapa
kids' triangle
courgettes and tomatoes
sweetcorn
Connie's sunflower
water tank

GOING STRAIGHT

Ok, you know what you want to grow, you have a rough idea of how to lay out your plot, and you've decided on raised beds, so the next question is: do you sow straight, or not? When you walk around allotment sites you'll see that most of the veg on the plot is sown and grown in straight lines; but the alternative for many crops is to scatter the seed within an area, otherwise known as broadcast sowing. There are advantages and disadvantages to both methods.

Straight lines look regimented and are easy to weed and hoe along. You know where the plants are, you can trace their development with no bother at all and you won't get your fellow plot holders leaning on their spades and asking unhelpful questions such as, 'what are you doing it like that for?'. It's also useful to sow in straight lines if you want to maximize your yield by planting catch crops between your slower-growing veg (see below).

Broadcast sowing, for example, with your carrot seeds (see page 68), gets a lot of seedlings in a lot less space, and although the roots may be smaller you will get more per square whatever measurement you care to choose than having gaps between individual plants. Broadcast sowing doesn't work for every crop, though – your caulis and cabbages really need that airy gap between plants – but for carrots, leeks, spring onions and salad crops, it is great. (My broadcast sown Parmex carrots were sensational. When we were filming for *Gardeners' World* I did actually taste them straight from the ground with only a sleeve wipe to clean them, but health and safety issues prevented that bit from being transmitted! They were great and I don't even really like carrots. The kids do, though.)

CATCH CROPS

Catch crops are fast maturing plants that can be grown between fully spaced vegetables, ensuring that the ground is used as productively as possible. Catch crops such as small lettuces, radishes, spring onions and spinach can easily be grown in between slower maturing plants such as potatoes, sweetcorn, cabbages and parsnips. They can be planted into the spaces between your main plants at the same time of planting, after the maincrop has gone in, or even after harvesting at the end of the season while the space is temporarily vacant. The most important thing to remember is not to grow anything that needs too long to mature, and to time it so the catch crop is harvested first, or before the maincrop needs the space to grow into.

Cover up

Once you've laid out the hard landscaping in your mind (or on paper), it's time to clear the plot in readiness for putting your plans into action.

You have two choices when first contemplating your plot: the first is to cultivate the whole thing; the second is to manage only part of the plot. What you decide to do depends on how much time you can dedicate to the plot, and how effective you are within that time. I got a lot of flak from dyed-in-the-wool allotment holders over working my whole plot in the first year, especially with the ever-present and robust horsetail. But in one-and-a-half days per week I can do a lot of weeding, sowing and planting, so I thought I'd give it a good go. Of course, however much of the plot you work at first shouldn't affect your overall plans; it's better to design the whole plot even if you are only using part of it at first, so as to save complications of design later.

If you honestly think it is too much to cope with to cultivate the whole plot at once, cover sections with black plastic or sow them with wildflower seeds. Black plastic will cook the weeds at the top, weaken any shoots and generally bring out any weeds near the surface, so you can remove them as and when you get round to planting up the area. Wildflowers and green manure (see page 172) make the plot look good (and I'm a great believer in making plots a place where you, your family and friends want to be) while also stopping a takeover bid from weeds. Covering up also prevents damage by rain; heavy rain on bare soil surfaces can result in nutrients being washed out, especially on lighter soils, and hard caps forming, which will require back-breaking digging at a later date to break up.

Clear up

A few days after the digger had scraped the allotment I went up to the plot to start digging it over. The soil was simply so dense and wet that every forkful was a real struggle. Having dug all my gardening life, I'll be honest and say that this was the hardest and slowest work I've taken on. After an hour or so of digging and weeding I looked back to see how much – or rather how little – I had done and decided that this simply wasn't the way to go. If I was there all week digging all day every day I wouldn't have cleared enough space to put in ten potatoes – and I didn't have a week!

Spraying off the weeds would have meant waiting until early spring in order to allow them to put on growth first, which would have meant I'd missed the boat for that year (not to mention the environmental and organic considerations such drastic action would have entailed).

If it had been a commercial landscaping job, I would have gone for the cheaper option of digging out all the weeds by machine and replacing the affected soil with imported topsoil, rather than hire labour to dig by hand to get it into good condition. This, obviously, wasn't a job on that scale, but it was starting to feel like it. So I took the decision to rotavate. I know this is now probably the most controversial decision ever made on *Gardeners' World*, and has been much documented, but I needed to get the soil into a state that I could put a fork into it, turn it over and incorporate some compost, too.

My soil desperately needed air and frost to help break it up and make it workable, and in order to expose it to these conditions, I needed to turn it over. So I hired a rotavator for one day the following week. It was a bright and sunny day with a strong breeze, which was perfect for drying out the soil quickly once the machine had broken it up. Every now and then I'd stop to examine the soil and could see lots of small, black, twig-like roots of the horsetail and knew it would be back with a vengeance.

Keith is retired and spends a lot more time on his plot than I do. He also opted to rotavate when he first took over and he's determined to get rid of his horsetail altogether.

Believe me, I knew exactly what I was doing and it was my choice to do it. I would pay for this decision all year, but at least it meant that for now I could move the soil and dig! I've been asked if I regret the decision; I say it was right for me and what I wanted to do at the time. For those who have more patience and aren't in a hurry to see quick returns on their allotment, digging by hand is probably the right option, but don't expect to see much from your plot in the first year or so, and if, like me, you have horsetail, no amount of digging will get rid of it because the roots go down forever!

My free scrape and rotavating experience is not necessarily the recommended way to clear a plot. The more formal, textbook ways include the following, but you need to do what you feel is right for you and your situation:

🍃 Hand dig small areas of the plot removing every scrap of weed root as you go. Whilst you are doing this it is advisable to cover any other unworked area with heavy-duty black plastic (avoid using blue tarpaulins – see page 134). This will keep weeds under control. I have to say this is the ideal way if you have the time and patience to work methodically through a plot. You might not get many crops in the first couple of years, but long term you will make life easier.

🍃 You could go down chemical alley and use glyphosate. I know many people want to grow their fruit and veg organically, so if this is the case (as it is for me), this option is out. But I also know and have seen fantastic plots where glyphosate is used to great effect. It is a personal choice and I'm not going to preach about organic methods or pesticides. I am growing organically, or without knowingly putting chemicals on the plot, but there are virtues in using glyphosate in certain situations.

Weeds

Ask any new allotment holder what is their biggest problem and 99 per cent of them will tell you it's the weeds. Weeds compete with your crops for the nutrients and moisture in the soil, and if left to their own devices will quickly colonize areas and smother crops.

The first thing to do is to identify what sort of weeds you have so that you know how to deal with them. Exactly what sort of weeds you get in your garden will depend to some extent on what sort of growing conditions you have.

KNOW YOUR WEEDS
1 Groundsel **2** Speedwell.
3 Chickweed **4** Sow thistle
5 Bindweed **6** Ground elder
7 Couch grass **8** Dandelion
9 Creeping buttercup

ANNUAL WEEDS

These germinate, mature and die away in one season, leaving behind them a supply of seed to germinate in the autumn or the following season. The seeds can lie in your soil for over 30 years and still germinate when they come to the surface, so you'll never eliminate them altogether. It's important to keep on top of them and remove them before they get a chance to set seed, but the good news is that they can usually be hoed over and left on top of the soil, ideally on a hot day, where they will dry out and die off immediately. Job done.

Annual weeds include: groundsel, common field speedwell, chickweed and sow thistle, amongst many others.

PERENNIAL WEEDS

Perennial weeds are far trickier customers as they will spread by seed, but also by creeping stems and invasive root systems which will re-grow if damaged or if part of them is left in the ground. It's important with perennial weeds that you dig out the whole plant with a fork or daisy grubber. Sometimes it's completely impossible to do this and some will be left in the ground to regenerate. In this case, all you can do is keep on top of them at every opportunity and they will get weaker and weaker over time. Perennial weeds include: bindweed, ground elder, couch grass, dandelions and creeping buttercup.

DISPOSING OF WEEDS

Some weeds are fine to put on the compost heap, but pick out the pernicious roots as, in my opinion, these are best kept off altogether. If in doubt, any weeds with seedheads can be put into a plastic bag and left on the top of the heap for a few weeks so that the heat will make them unviable. Remember the old adage too: one year's seeding means seven years' weeding – so don't allow your weeds to set seed. If the seeds are right on the cusp of dispersal, walk round with a paper bag and snap off the seedheads into the bag before they end up all over your plot, and keep the seeds off your compost heap.

The allotmenteers' way to clear a plot

So how do the experts clear the plot? I've chatted with fellow allotment holders and in doing so have gleaned a whole load of tips. Some, I have to say, we wouldn't put out on air. (This is mainly because of rules and regulations surrounding home-made concoctions to get rid of weeds. I can't suggest you use something to kill horsetail if that product, whatever it is, isn't marketed specifically to kill horsetail.)

So here a few of the allotment holders' ways of getting rid of weeds and of clearing a plot of anything and everything. I haven't tried any of them, so I can't guarantee they will work and I am certainly not saying you have to use them. (There, that's the lawyer happy!)

Cardboard. Yes, thick layers of cardboard laid on top of soil will kill off weeds. The added bonus to this method is that if you leave it there, the cardboard will rot down. (Although I do worry about chemicals in the cardboard, as a lot of glue is used in its manufacture.) To stop cardboard blowing away, put a thick layer of manure on top. I like this idea (even with the reservations about chemicals), as the person who told me explained that it makes pulling any weeds out really easy and the worms love it.

Black plastic is used in most allotment sites to smother weeds. This makes sense, because it excludes the light while also encouraging high temperatures. I tried a few sheets on a spare piece of the allotment (the bit at the top near Keith's chickens) and it did discourage weeds, but the side effect was it was a perfect breeding ground for slugs. Still, whipping the sheet away in the morning gave the local birds a chance of an early morning feed, and Keith's chickens go berserk for slugs.

Vinegar was mentioned on my blog and subsequent enquiries have shown that lots of you use it as a weedkiller. The idea is that neat household vinegar, poured or sprayed directly onto weeds, will and does kill them. It works on young weeds, but my older horsetail laughs in the face of acetic acid. I believe higher concentrations of vinegar are available but they can be dangerous, so leave well alone.

Salt does a similar thing to vinegar and is most effective in strong sunlight. A spray or wash is the best way to apply salt solution. With home-made salt and vinegar solutions it is best to add some washing up liquid, as this will ensure the solution doesn't form big drops and merely run off the leaves before the salt or vinegar has a chance to kill the plant.

GLYPHOSATE – TO SPRAY OR NOT TO SPRAY?

When you stand, spade in hand, in front of your new plot that's full of weeds, I can forgive you for thinking 'Lets reach for the weedkiller'. I know, I had the same thought, too. There are some pretty nasty chemicals out there, but the one that a lot of gardeners use contains glyphosate, as it is considered by many to be the safest chemical around.

Glyphosate works on green and any soft plant material – and that's anything green or soft. Councils use it a lot around trees; the tree trunks don't get affected, but the weeds do. The neat trick is that once in the plant, glyphosate travels through the entire plant system, killing as it goes. The point being that a spray on the leaves kills the entire plant.

It's all well and good to say it only kills green tissue, which it does, but while you are spraying willy-nilly to, say, rid yourself of a patch of bindweed, you may also be killing off other more desirable plants that you want in your display, or that might be home to wildlife.

The manufacturers state that glyphosate is safe to use and that once the chemical comes into contact with the soil it is deactivated. What happens is that the microbial activity in the soil breaks it down. I did a bit of research into glyphosate and everything said about it is correct, but research is ongoing and it has been shown to cause damage to lab rats in high doses and frequency.

True, we would never get that kind of dosage or activity, but there's something I'm not sure about. It isn't just the actual glyphosate that worries me; what you are using is actually a cocktail of chemicals, some of which are present to ensure the glyphosate sticks to the leaves. It may well get absorbed onto the soil particles and it may well get broken down by bacteria and fungi, and it may well say it is safe to use on here, there and everywhere, but … maybe a spade and fork are best. It may take longer, but at least I know I haven't added anything to the soil.

If you do decide to use it, do so carefully. Remember, it will kill anything that is green. Two tips passed on to me by fellow plot holders are to crush stems of woodier plants (and I include horsetail in that bracket) before spraying and to place a large plastic bottle with the base cut out over the offending plant and spray into that. The bottle will stop any spray drifting on to desirable plants nearby.

So, you see, there is a much bigger picture than the patch of weed in front of your eyes – but I promised not to preach …

Intro to landscaping

Some allotment holders like to build permanent and semi permanent structures into their plots by introducing landscaped elements. These can be anything from a simple path or raised beds to more complex constructions, such as sheds or fruit cages. Although they do take up time and possibly money at the start, they should be a worthwhile investment because they make the allotment more organised, practical, and less maintenance-hungry. They will often increase the yields of your crops too.

Be sure to focus the effort you put in by planning carefully before embarking on a project. If you don't have any prior landscaping experience, the allotment is the ideal place to have a go at it. Have fun, be imaginative and resourceful, and look to recycle wherever possible. But don't get caught up with putting landscaped areas in if you don't want to. I have seen some wonderful plots that have absolutely no permanent structures at all – the paths are simply consolidated soil between the beds; the climbing structures are seasonal and temporary; and in the winter most of the plot will be taken back to a simple strip of empty soil.

RAISED BEDS

When it came to my raised beds, this was another of my controversial decisions. I decided to construct my now-famous triangular- and diamond-shaped raised beds. The idea came about from the free wood I managed to salvage from a local DIY store. Many people think that I somehow 'persuaded' them to give it to me as I was the bloke on the telly, but they were honestly throwing it all away as it was twisted and had gone silver so they couldn't sell it. I didn't want to cut the timbers up so I devised a layout of raised beds that meant I could use them as whole pieces.

The day that Peter Whiting, Allotment Holder of the Year 2007, came to visit me was the day I had laid them out. I asked him if he thought they would work well, or was I perhaps getting a bit fancy? He said they'd be good for a crop rotation system.

When I placed them over the soil, the whole plot came together; immediately making it look organized so that I could finally see where I was heading. I thought the diamonds and triangles would also look dynamic on the site, would divide the space into more manageable areas, and would personalize it for me. Ken, a fellow plotholder, thought I'd completely lost the plot and was laying out a Hampton Court Flower Show exhibit, but looking back, I'm glad I did it and I wouldn't have done it any other way.

····}

Raised beds have several advantages and I would recommend building some if you can. As soon as Peter and I placed the boards on the plot to form my now legendary diamonds and triangles, it immediately made the huge expanse of soil feel manageable.

PROS AND CONS OF RAISED BEDS
Pros
⬤ Reduced soil compaction from not stepping on the planting areas means that the plant roots get plenty of air which encourages fast growth.

⬤ Plants can be grown closer together as you don't need paths or spaces to tread. Do be careful of over-crowding your plants though, as they tend to grow larger in raised beds.

⬤ Increased drainage means they are ideal on heavy soils and most edibles grow far better on free-draining soils.

⬤ The soil will warm up quicker in the spring, meaning any plants you grow will be a step ahead of those grown at ground level.

⬤ Compost and fertilizer can be applied more accurately and carefully.

⬤ They are easier to garden as they are closer to you, and help to avoid too much bending over.

⬤ They help you to organize your site and add some permanence to the layout.

Cons
⬤ More permanent – if you build them with a timber retaining edge they are a pain to move around and you'll need to change the soil levels.

⬤ They're the ideal hiding place for slugs and snails.

A PLACE FOR THE KIDS

I've always wanted the kids to have their very own garden area that they could do exactly what they wanted with and dig, plant and get really muddy. The allotment provided no shortage of space to let them loose on, but I didn't want to overwhelm them either, so my plan was to start them off by giving them a triangle to share. As they had more allotment experience than me from their visits to 'Nanny' Brenda's plot, they took to it like ducks to water. It's interesting how they both approach it: Connie using her artistic eye and making it look great, whereas Stanley just loves to dig and has been extremely useful fetching and barrowing the council compost.

A PLACE FOR THE GROWN-UPS (WELL, MEN...)

The humble shed. Yeah, I know, men and their sheds! But, being a bit of a bloke, I have always wanted my own shed. I don't have one at home as I store my tools in the cellar, but from day one of deciding to get an allotment I had visualized sitting in my shed having a cup of tea, while looking out and surveying my plot. On a practical level, it's also extremely useful to keep things dry such as seeds, tools and, of course, tea bags, and a lovely place to pot up plants. Of course, as I've already said, if it rains when we're filming the expensive camera and sound equipment are the first, and the kids love to muck about in it too. I had to apply in writing to be allowed to put it up (see page 25).

Of course, I couldn't buy a brand new shed – it would have cost the equivalent of a year's rent and have looked all wrong anyway. I asked around a few friends to see if anyone had one going, but no joy, so I decided to look online and see if there were any going locally (I didn't want to be trekking around London on a wild shed chase). Well, I got my little eight by four foot (2.4 x 1.2 metre) beauty for £26. It was in panels and the price didn't include delivery, so I called on my good old friend and shed-lover Cleve West (he has three on his allotments) to help me out.

When we saw it the floor was completely rotten so I knocked the seller down to a bargain £25 and he also threw in some old doors he was chucking away, which would make a decent floor and a potting table. We took it straight to the allotment and put it up in a very Laurel and Hardy way. We used some old pallets as a base and it went up in no time. I even forgot to put the roof on first time around. I strided off up the path thinking we were finished and forgetting the shed was still open to the elements with Cleve still in it. Talk about Laurel and Hardy – this was more Buster Keaton!

I placed it at the top end of the site in a shady spot by the tree. It was

to become the amenity area of the layout, near the compost bins.
I replaced the dodgy-looking glass windows with some clear plastic for
the kids' safety, knocked up the potting table out of one of the old doors
and, hey presto, the plot now looked like home!

I was now in complete allotment mode – frugal and looking to recycle
whatever I could get my hands on. The next week I used some leftover
pallets to make a decked veranda (sounds fancy, eh?) around the shed
by simply placing the wood on landscape fabric and nailing the pallets
together to stop them flipping up. I then threw some of the composted
bark donated by the tree surgeons into the gaps to make an even surface.

What a beauty! As well as
all the practical uses of the
shed for storage and keeping
us dry, it also helps to give
my plot its own identity.

Soil testing

I strongly recommend that, before taking on a plot, you plunge your spade into the soil to check out exactly what you've got. Soil type varies from site to site, and even from plot to plot. This knowledge will influence what kind of veg you can grow successfully, and it also gives you the starting point from which you can improve your soil and get the most from your plot.

CLAY SOIL – sticky to handle and a chunk of the stuff can be compressed into a solid ball. I read somewhere that clay soil is 'difficult to dig'; difficult is an understatement. You really have to time your gardening on a heavy clay soil. In summer, or at least the summers I remember as a kid, it bakes rock hard and cracks appear on its surface. In winter, or recent summers, it quickly becomes too heavy to work in serious rain. It also seems to take ages to warm up in spring, making it necessary to delay sowing and planting. The upside is that this kind of soil contains plenty of nutrients and, once worked and treated with tonnes of organic matter, it is great at holding enough moisture to produce fantastic yields.

SANDY SOIL – grab a handful and try and make a ball. No chance. It is gritty and sandy to feel and it drains like a colander. This soil will never waterlog, but when the sun shines and the rain stops your plants will gasp for water. It also loses most of its nutrients quickly, so you will be bulking up and watering for most of your spare days at your plot. This time the upside is that it warms up quickly in spring so you can be off to a flying start, and it is so easy to dig you will never have a wasted trip to the plot.

LOAMY SOIL – the Holy Grail of all allotment holders. Imagine the best of all worlds: a soil that holds moisture yet never becomes waterlogged; a soil that holds nutrients and warms up quickly in spring; a workable soil almost every day of the year; a soil that is light and easy to dig. It does exist, but, sadly, I cannot claim such a soil. You could strike lucky and get a plot with a loamy soil, or if you have the time and inclination, you can work the soil into something resembling loam. This will take tonnes of muck and compost and hours of digging, but the results are worth it.

SILTY SOIL – usually deposited by rivers, these soils are silky to the touch and great for growing veg. They contain more nutrients than sandy soils and drain better than clay, but if they are deposited by rivers the chances

LAYING A PATHWAY
1 Once you've planned the area for your pathway, level out the ground around it and roll out the landscape fabric. **2** Cut the fabric to fit the area you want to cover. **3** You'll need something durable to pin down the fabric. I use heavy gauge galvanised wire for pins. **4** Pin through the fabric into the ground. **5** You can use bark, chippings, gravel or whatever over the fabric to make it look more attractive. **6** Rake out to cover the fabric evenly.

are that the same river is nearby, so you'll need to check with the council about flooding. It can be heartbreaking to see your plot under water after prolonged heavy rain.

PEATY SOIL – this does actually exist and is darker in colour, holds loads of water and can be bone dry in summer. There is also a bit of an acidity issue with high peat content: some veg will react against acidity. In its favour, it does warm up quickly, so sowing and planting can be done early.

CHALKY SOIL – in winter, wrists are strained as you strike clumps of chalk when digging, and in summer your biceps ache due to the gallons of water you have to carry to rehydrate parched plants (the same plants that look sickly because of nutrient deficiency). It makes you glad to have a clay soil – sometimes. Again, barrow loads of organic matter will help, but don't entertain the thought of getting rid of that chalk. You can fight nature, but you will never beat it.

KNOW YOUR PH LEVEL

Knowing the structure of your soil is one aspect of growing veg, but another is knowing the pH level – the measure of how acidic or alkaline the soil is. Soil science is a complex subject so, to put it simply, the pH determines the amounts of specific nutrients that are made available to your plants. Certain pH's lock up nutrients, which means the plants tend to look hungry or ill. And that's what you need to know as an allotment holder. So it is, therefore, well worth getting to know the pH of your soil.

A soil testing kit will easily and cheaply do this for you. They are available from nurseries and garden centres. Once purchased, it's usually just a case of taking a soil sample, adding a drop or two of water along with the 'magic' tablet, shaking, waiting, and then comparing the colour of the resultant suspension to the chart provided in the pack.

That done, you'll soon know your pH level. If it's 7, it is slap bang neutral, which is in the middle and spot-on for growing 99 per cent of veg. A pH of below 7 means your soil is acidic and will be great for radishes, swedes and turnips, although you might want to bring the pH nearer to neutral to support more than just these root crops, as they will still grow happily at pH 7. A pH of above 7 means your soil is alkaline and your brassicas will be spectacular show-winners. Too high up this scale, though, and you might start locking some nutrients up, so you should think about bringing the pH back towards neutral by adding well-rotted manure or sulphur.

Planning your planting

A common complaint amongst new allotment holders is that you wait around for months then everything crops at the same time. Usually when you are on holiday. The way around this is to plan what you are going to grow very carefully so that you stagger the amounts of seed you sow or plants you put in, sowing and planting a few at a time, leaving a fortnight and popping a few more in. The key thing to remember is that staggering the starting point of crops that have similar germination and cropping times usually results in staggered harvesting.

Another way of avoiding gluts is to sow earlier and later. Of course, if the soil isn't warm enough, this is not possible, but a few craftily placed cloches will warm it up and get things going. A greenhouse or polytunnel is a better option, but at the moment that's just a dream of mine.

One allotment holder told me that using different varieties of the same type of veg is best, as they will mature at different rates. It was such a good idea he swapped half a packet of his carrot seed (I think it was Autumn King) for half of my Flyaway.

Crop rotation

I think everyone on *Gardeners' World* has had a go at explaining crop rotation at some point or another, but on screen it always looks difficult.

The reason gardeners rotate their crops is to keep the soil in tip-top condition, thereby getting the best out of their plants. The great allotment gardener Peter Whiting came down to my plot and explained the whole thing to me; the basic idea is that you never grow the same crop in the same piece of soil for four years. The reasoning behind this is that a plant takes nutrients out of the soil, and if grown in the same spot year after year the roots will extract the same nutrients until, pretty soon, the soil becomes exhausted.

Pests and diseases rear their collective ugly head at this point. Crops get attacked by stuff, it comes with the territory, and if the same plant is planted in the same soil year on year you could get a build up of a particular pest or disease, which very quickly will cause big problems. You still with me?

There's one more point to remember: the way you cultivate some crops makes the soil perfect the following year for another type of crop, and some crops even make natural nutrients for the following crop to come along and use. For example, brassicas, as hungry plants, should follow legumes.

I'll try to explain this more clearly in a table. First, divide your plot into four or more sections (I used five). Then classify your crops into these groups:

A. Legumes: all your peas and beans
B. Brassicas: cabbage, cauliflowers, calabrese, broccoli, radish, swede
C. Onions: including shallots, leeks and garlic
D. Potato family: including potatoes (naturally enough) and tomatoes
E. Umbellifers: such as carrots, parsnips, celery and fennel

Over the next five years you should grow the following crops in the following sections of your plot:

	Section 1	Section 2	Section 3	Section 4	Section 5
Year 1	A	B	C	D	E
Year 2	B	C	D	E	A
Year 3	C	D	E	A	B
Year 4	D	E	A	B	C
Year 5	E	A	B	C	D

Most other crops aren't too fussy about crop rotation, so you can grow them wherever you have space, year after year. This applies to chicory, courgettes, lettuce, marrows, peppers, pumpkins, squashes and sweetcorn.

Nitrogen fixing

This can be complicated and will bore the socks off anyone who isn't heavily into soil science (my feet are suddenly very cold), but it is important information if you want to get a really good harvest. There is, in fact, a short and snappy explanation of nitrogen fixing and why you should look at your pea and bean plants in a completely different way.

◗ Plants need nitrogen for healthy growth, but mainly for leaf production.
◗ There's loads of nitrogen in the air but plants can't get it and use it, so

they have evolved a method of trapping, or 'fixing' it from forms of
nitrogen 'stored' in the actual soil.

⬤ Naturally occurring bacteria in the soil (mostly rhizobium) 'infect' roots
of legumes and when in the root hairs, they multiply and cause swellings
or nodules to develop. (You can buy these rhizobium from garden centres.)
Complex chemical reactions take place in these swellings and the nitrogen
is fixed in the soil and made available to plants in the form of ammonia.

⬤ When the roots die off at the end of the season, they leave behind the
fixed ammonia, leaving you with free fertilizer.

⬤ Three cheers for legumes and maybe four cheers for rhizobium.

So, the message is, don't bother with nitrogen fertilizers and don't whatever
you do entirely rip out your plants once they have died. You need to let
those nodules rot away in the soil if they are to release that wonderful,
natural, free fertilizer. So when plants are finished, cut the top growth off
and put it on the compost heap (shred or chop it up first to give it a chance
of breaking down quickly), then dig any roots that have lifted during the
dig back into the soil.

Organic fertilizers

I firmly believe that if you get the soil in good shape you won't need to
feed your plants. The answer does lie in the soil. But sometimes it will
need a boost and I am determined not to use any chemical fertilizers on
the plot. It's personal but given this chance to grow organically I might
as well try. I believe artificial fertilizers will boost growth and that makes
plants susceptible to pests and diseases. Monty Don always says to grow
your plants hard. Of course, choosing to add fertilizer or not is your choice.
I do occasionally like to add calcified seaweed to the crops. This stuff
encourages loads of microbial activity in the soil and helps the strength
of plants. Old fashioned blood, fish and bone is a great general fertilizer –
I use it instead of Growmore. Tomato fertilizers are rich in potash and good
for boosting fruit and tomatoes. Most are chemicals but there are organic
tomato fertilizers available. Otherwise I haven't bought any packeted or
liquid fertilizers. Get that soil right and the crops will look after themselves.
It's good gardening practice and sound financial advice.

Joe's Veg Heroes
Cleve West

Cleve West is a garden designer and writer and has won many RHS awards including three gold medals at the RHS Chelsea Flower Show. He's also a good friend of mine and we always have a laugh together. As well as being someone I can phone any time for advice, he's also pretty handy, so I roped him into helping me put up my shed at the allotment!

Cleve West

Allotment Hampton Court, Surrey. 4 plots totalling 30 rods. (plus 3 sheds, 1 greenhouse)

Soil type Sandy/neutral

Annual rent £160

Biggest growing problem Protecting plants against slugs, as we don't like to kill them. In fact, we don't like to kill anything, which obviously causes problems because the pests see our plot as the one offering free meals!

Favourite tool I like my onion hoe because it looks like a proper tool, but I'd say a circle hoe is probably my most efficient tool.

Favourite crop They're all good, but if I had to pick one thing it would be potatoes. Cooked within minutes of being dug up, they're hard to beat. I love my fresh peas, too.

Favourite time of year I love winter because it's the time that you get loads done, as things slow down and you can start to take complete control again. It also looks like you've done something, but at the same time there are still plenty of vegetables to pick and take home at the end of the day.

What's your first memory of vegetable growing? Eating strawberries in my grandparents' garden and at the same time disturbing a wasp's nest and getting stung. I can also remember buying seed potatoes instead of proper potatoes for supper one day, so I decided to plant them rather than eat them and while doing so dug up a hibernating tortoise. What a disaster!

When did you first grow vegetables? In 2000 I got an allotment to grow veg because my garden was too small. I was also becoming increasingly concerned about what was going into the food that I was eating, and I wanted to be in control. I don't fully trust organically labelled food at the supermarket, so I wanted to grow my own and know precisely what had gone into it.

Why do you love your allotment? As I'm a garden designer and always in front of a computer or meeting up with clients, in fact it's the only real gardening I get to do these days. I also love the camaraderie of the allotment and generally being outdoors in the fresh air. I was a pretty good athlete when I was younger and need regular exercise, which I certainly get at the plot. There's also no doubt the food tastes far better when eaten fresh.

What do you do with your excess produce? Give it all to friends.

What is the best piece of growing advice you've ever been given? Take your time. Don't be tempted to plant too early on in the year – and protect everything!

What's the best advice you can give to other growers? Don't take on too big a plot to begin with, and lower your expectations of what you might produce in your first year.

Spring at the plot

Once I'd got started, spring seemed to take forever to arrive. I was still going up to the allotment at every opportunity, which was mainly on weekends as the days were short. I would dig for hours and hours to try to get the soil into some sort of reasonable state to plant, but I was seriously up against it. Weed roots were coming out by the bucketful. Fortunately, there were a few late winter frosts that helped to break up the soil, making it more workable. When I wasn't digging, or if the ground was simply too wet, I worked on the infrastructure by putting down paths, building my compost heaps and stockpiling some of the council compost for later on.

I was desperate to get some things into the ground, just to make a start and so that I could fill up some of the enormous areas of bare soil, but I knew I needed to be patient because the soil was still far too cold. I bought a load of different onions, garlic and shallot sets and started them off in small pots and cells. Most of the other plot holders had plenty already coming on nicely from their autumn-planted varieties, so I felt as if I was behind already. But just getting these plants going felt good, and it felt like I'd made a small breakthrough.

I ordered plenty of potatoes to chit too, which again proved to be a bit of a hassle as it was too warm inside and too dark in the cellar. They like a light, dry, cool, but frost-free, position so I bought some cheap, clear storage boxes and put them into those, and then placed them in the garden, letting fresh air in every day or so. Looking back it does seem a little over the top now – it was like having dozens of small children to look after!

I did leave one bag of potatoes in the cellar, though, and completely forgot about them. I had a bit of a shock when I did eventually remember them as they had very long shoots coming off them like dreadlocks. I didn't plant them but I reckon if I'd rubbed off the shoots and put them in, they'd probably have come up okay, as spuds are tough as old boots and, like most plants, just want to grow.

Spring is the time of year when plot holders take a very keen interest in the weather, as it can literally change hourly from warm sunshine to frosts and snow. As well as tuning into the weather I made sure I was tuned into the radio too. Not for the footy scores this time, but for the daily weather forecast!

The busiest time of the year

Even with successional sowing and planting (sowing half a row one week, leaving it a fortnight or so and sowing some more so that plants mature at different times and you don't get gluts), it is inevitable that spring is the busiest time of the year on the allotment. You seem to wait weeks to get going, with all your plans on paper, and then suddenly it is a case of playing catch up as spring races away. And of course while all your much-cherished seeds are going in, that dreaded horsetail is breaking through again. My one day per week at the plot was, and is, about a seventh of what I really needed to be doing.

My biggest piece of advice to any new plot holder is not to panic. It is not a race. Some of your allotment neighbours may well pride themselves on getting the first potato shoots up, or the first spindly, almost fragile, row of carrot seedlings showing through, but it shouldn't bother you. It did me, though.

Being new to the whole scene and having the added hassle of sometimes having to wait for a film crew to get there, I frequently had to delay sowing and planting. But you know something? I was glad. In a wet, cold spring, seeds will just sit in the soil and at best lie dormant, at worse rot away. Potato shoots may well herald that the growing season is underway, but unless you live close to your plot they will be frosted without the overnight protection of hessian or paper, and that paper has to be removed by mid-morning the next day. No – delay a little and lie in bed knowing there will be a happy ending.

Sowing under cover

Any cover provides protection. It may be the cover of a greenhouse, your house or cloches, but it will extend the season by a few weeks. Some crops, such as aubergines, need a long growing season and are best sown early, indoors, on a bright windowsill, and can be planted out in your allotment when summer comes (you might have trouble with these if you try to grow them in the north. They're more suited to warmer, southern plots). Ken did this and has had a great crop this year. He did the same with a lot of chilli peppers, too.

Back home I don't have a greenhouse, or even a windowsill, as my kitchen has glass doors that span right across the back of the house and down to ground level. I needed somewhere to get seedlings going, so my solution was to buy a simple, cheap, and easy-to-make plastic shelf system, which I put against the window indoors and filled with pots that I'd sown seeds into. It was so exciting to see the first shoots of the courgettes, squashes and tomatoes coming up. Growing from seed is a wonderful thing to do, and it always amazes me what a tiny seed can produce. The first thing the kids and I would do in the morning was check to see if anything had germinated or put on growth.

There was a slight flaw in this plan, in that my kitchen has underfloor heating and because it's south facing it gets plenty of sun. I was concerned that the seedling plants were going to bolt and get leggy, as they were going pretty much straight from a dormant state to the warm, bright, midsummer conditions that the indoor environment created. I started keeping a close eye on the weather forecast and taking the seedlings in and out of the garden to slow them down when it wasn't too cold. It was a right old fiddle to be honest, but it was the only thing I could do, given the circumstances.

I didn't discover the joys of a cloche until autumn. Next spring I'm planning on having cold frames and a polytunnel or two up at the allotment, which would certainly help, but now I can see why a frost-free greenhouse is every serious veg grower's dream. One consideration with any form of cover is watering. On a warm sunny day the soil in pots under cover can dry out extremely quickly. This is okay if you've got your little babies at home, but another thing to think about if your allotment is further away like mine is.

The trick with growing seedlings indoors, I have discovered, is not to leave them there for too long. All seedlings want to do is grow, and they do that quickly because of the higher temperatures, but unfortunately the light levels in spring are not high enough to sustain solid growth. What you get is long, etiolated or stringy seedlings that never really turn into good plants. Plan ahead, sow later than your instinct tells you and you won't go far wrong. I also saw in one allotmenteer's greenhouse a row of trays crammed full of seedlings, with a backing board lined with tinfoil. The idea behind this was that tinfoil reflects back any available light to prevent this unwanted stretching of seedlings. I suppose on the same basis you could also paint the board white.

Hardening off

It's one of those great gardening terms, and one that you will frequently hear down at the allotment. 'Are they hardened off?' All it means is: have you acclimatised the plants you have been growing under protection to the great outdoors?

To do that, you just put the trays outside in a warm, sheltered position during the day and bring them back indoors at night. Do this for a fortnight or so, avoiding any severe weather and your plants will romp away and not sulk (like my peppers did) when they are eventually permanently planted out after all risk of frost is passed. As far as possible, you should always time this hardening off to avoid the worst of the weather.

If your plants are growing in a cold frame, just leave the glass tops open during the day and close them up in the late afternoon or early evening. Again, a fortnight of doing this will help the development of the plant and ready it for facing the big wide world outdoors.

1 Exotic aubergines will need plenty of protection from the erratic spring temperatures, but they can sit happily in the sun on a warm day. **2** Although brassicas such as these caulis are tough, young plants still need the opportunity to adjust to outside temperatures before being planted out.

Crops to sow indoors in spring

Once spring had sprung, it was time for me to get sowing and planting at last. Here are a few crops that you need to get going under cover so they're ready to plant out as the days get warmer and the frosts have passed.

AUBERGINES

They are a bit of a gamble outdoors, but if the summer is warm and you can protect growing plants from any cold winds, you should get a decent crop. Look out for a variety called Diamond, as it crops relatively quickly from a sowing in March. Other varieties can take too long to flower and so will never develop fruit in an average, short British summer.

CAULIFLOWERS, CALABRESE AND CABBAGE

All these can be sown directly outside in spring, but I started mine off in 9 cm pots filled with peat-free multipurpose compost because I wanted to get a head start on the awful spring that was occurring outdoors. I sowed three seeds per pot as they are quite large and easy to handle. A cover of clingfilm kept things moist, and within ten days my first brassica seedlings made an appearance. I grew them on, hardened them off and planted them out in May.

My cauliflower was All the Year Round; it is a well-known and popular variety that promised large white heads of tasty cauliflower. It delivered. The calabrese I grew was Typhoon. This was a great variety, producing masses of dark green spears that the kids adored. I grew a few cabbage plants of the variety Primo, too, which all produced small but rock solid heads in September.

PEPPERS

I tried growing some chilli peppers from seed and I have to say they were good. The heat of a chilli pepper is in the seed, so be careful when handling them, even at sowing time. I did find germination a bit hit and miss; I sowed five seeds each into a couple of pots and only got four plants in total. It was enough, though, and I duly pricked them out into containers, grew them on, hardened them off and planted them out into a corner of one of the diamond-shaped beds on the allotment in late spring.

Maybe they were surprised at being planted out, as they seemed to sulk for a month, but they eventually got growing and produced a decent crop. Stan, my son, was up at the plot and decided to have a bite out of one of

them. He dared me to do the same, so obviously I took up the challenge. They were hot. They were really hot. We both had tears streaming down our faces and the bottled water we'd brought to drink did no good to ease what was rapidly developing into pain. Apparently milk or yoghurt is the best remedy to counteract the heat.

I also grew a milder, orange cayenne pepper. I have to say that they are also gorgeous plants to look at. Next year I'll sow more, and maybe this time in pots. Someone told me that if you grow peppers in pots, and grow them really hard – and they meant almost letting them wilt before watering – it will produce even stronger tasting peppers. However, after this year's experience I'm not sure I need them any stronger, thank you very much.

TOMATOES

My whole family loves tomatoes, and a few outdoor plants were supposed to provide us with off-the-vine snacks when we were all up there and maybe a little extra to make passata when we got home.

It was going well. I sowed seeds in trays in April, a little later than some, but I was running out of space on the windowsill and the BBC wanted to film it for a programme in April. I did the usual pricking out, hardening off, planting into one of the diamonds, this time through weed suppressant membrane as the weeds were beginning to get on my nerves. With plenty of water and a cane for support, a few fruits appeared, but I guessed the heaviest crop would be waiting for us on our return from holiday. However, blight had different ideas. Almost overnight it struck the whole country and complete plants were blackened, rendering affected fruits useless. Still, there's always next year.

I tried to grow Gartenperle for the promise of hundreds of small, tasty fruits (and the seeds were free on the front of a well-known gardening magazine). It is a self-branching variety and great for containers and even hanging baskets. I fancied them tumbling over the edges of my raised beds. I also had a go with Marmande, as I like the larger beefsteak varieties. All were struck down by blight.

Next year I might play safe and grow a variety called Legend. It should produce heavy crops of juicy fruits on bushy plants that are resistant to tomato blight. We'll see.

It may be cheaper to grow your own young plants from seedlings, but many garden centres these days will sell pots of veggie plants ready to plant straight out in spring, which is the route some of the plot holders on my site take.

Joe's Veg Heroes
Joy Larkcom

Joy Larkcom is Britain's most respected vegetable-garden maker and writer. She has travelled extensively in the USA, Europe and China researching plants, and is the author of *Grow Your Own Vegetables*, *The Organic Salad Garden* and *Creative Vegetable Gardening*. Joy encourages people to be adventurous about what they grow and not to be put off by having a small plot.

Joy Larkcom

Veg garden West Cork, southern Ireland, near the sea. The whole property (including all buildings) is about half an acre. Vegetables probably occupy around 30 square metres.

Soil type Very fertile, alkaline, well drained, slatey loam.

Biggest growing problem Slugs, and the damage from exposure to salt winds, which can literally tear off rhubarb and chard leaves, and even uproot winter cauliflowers.

Time spent on vegetable growing Probably about an hour a day, but my husband does all the heavy work.

Favourite tool A short-handled Chinese hoe, rather like an onion hoe, made from an old saw. It's part rake, part hoe, and I use it for all my sowings of cut-and-come-again seedlings, which is the backbone of my veg growing.

Favourite crop Everything is good at its peak, and especially if it's the first of the season: the first spuds, first peas, asparagus, first tomatoes, winter pumpkins; and my great love, a stir fry of oriental greens!

Favourite time of year Probably spring when the whole sowing cycle starts again; but the 'fullness' of summer is lovely.

What's your first memory of vegetable growing? My father returning from the war and digging up the garden we'd moved to in Berkshire, and giving me the wireworms to feed the hens.

When did you first grow vegetables? I first grew vegetables seriously, in my own garden, when I was married and the first baby arrived, which was in my thirties, though our family had always grown their own.

Why do you love growing fruit and vegetables so much? My first love was trees, and then fruit, and the greatest challenge, and greatest reward in this retirement garden in West Cork is growing fruit – soft fruit and top fruit. I do now have a succession of fruit for breakfast for eight or nine months in the year, and it probably gives me more pleasure than any other aspect of the garden. And of course I do still grow lots of vegetables, and the urge to experiment dies hard, though there is less space, and, critically, less energy to do this than before. I'm also still obsessed

with the concept of making veg gardens beautiful and integrating vegetables with non-edible crops.

Why do you think growing your own is important? There is something enormously rewarding about producing your own food. Then there are certainly some vegetables that taste so much better when home-grown (not all of them), and once you have experienced that, it's hard to go back to shop-bought. Obviously, I think that from a world point of view, if everyone stopped eating meat and put the ground saved to vegetable production, many of the current problems would be solved, so growing vegetables is important. I think growing anything – not necessarily vegetables – is very therapeutic and satisfying, and it is great to introduce kids to those pleasures that can remain with them for life.

What do you do with excess produce? Before we retired we had an experimental market garden, and so we sold excess produce. Now we have less space, there is very little excess, not least because I try to follow my own advice and sow little and often.

What's the best advice you can give to other growers? Probably be observant above all. Watch what is happening; spot pest damage or other damage before it becomes serious. See what does well where. Keep notes. Be humble … you never know it all and are always learning something new.

Sowing outdoors

When the soil eventually warmed up around mid-spring I planted out the onions, garlic and shallots into one half of a diamond. They lined up pretty well into a triangle shape as I offset them.

This was when the experience of my fellow allotmenteers began to be a huge help. Peter gave me some good advice, he suggested I plant them nice and deep to stop the birds pulling at their tops thinking they're worms. Manuel had just dug up twenty or so of his good-sized garlic plants and he gave them to me right there and then. I felt rather embarrassed as he was giving me loads of his prized produce, but he insisted I had them, saying he wanted to make room for other crops.

Of course, I put them straight into my beds and it felt fantastic to finally have some plants in the ground. I was so pleased with myself. I wouldn't have anything to eat from the allotment for a long time, but I had started the cycle. The theory was that all I had to do with that piece of planted ground now was to weed and water, which meant I could now move on to another patch and get that planted up, too.

I also dug a big pit for my beans and peas and filled it with cardboard, old paper, grass clippings, etc., and then backfilled it with topsoil (see page 186). Sounds an odd thing to do? Well it's because they are hungry plants which need plenty of moisture, so they benefit from this process because all this mulching helps retain water. It was of benefit to me, too, as there's nothing better than hard digging on a cold day to warm yourself up!

The bamboo wigwams for the peas and the double rows of bamboo canes for the beans added instant height to the plot. This may sound silly, but the structures immediately made it look like a proper allotment. The support was all there and ready for me to sow my peas and beans directly into the soil as it was warming up.

On that day Keith whipped out some globe artichoke plants that he didn't want and offered them to me. As well as loving the fruit, I think they're beautiful plants. They have a long tap root and as they drooped they looked extremely sad, but I've been patient with them and they now look healthy again, so I've high hopes of getting something off them next year.

···⟩

1 My French beans were sown directly into the ground and came up in no time. **2** Manuel's garlic looked perfectly at home in a corner of one of the triangles. **3** I started these onions off in pots and once the soil had warmed up I planted them into a raised bed. **4** My first row of early potatoes just had to be Swifts, and it was a joy to see their shoots breaking through the soil.

Crops to sow outdoors in spring

As the soil warms up and the days get longer, you can at last get a few crops sown directly into the soil. This is the best way of growing crops that don't like being moved later on, such as root crops like carrots, and saves you the time and space of sowing into lots of pots and transplanting.

CARROTS

I sowed these seeds successively in small blocks throughout late spring, once the soil had warmed up a bit, through to the end of summer. I just raked over a small area of bed, scattered the carrot seed and sprinkled bagged compost on top.

Just using a light covering ensured the compost didn't form a hard pan over the developing seedlings and it also marked the area so I could keep an eye on it for weeds. The feathery tops of carrot seedlings are distinct from my usual bindweed, horsetail and couch grass. Carrot fly is the major problem with this crop (see page 96), but the second is related, and comes from sowing too thickly. Too many seedlings mean you need to thin them out by removing several to give the others space to grow, and by doing this you not only waste seed, but also the scent of the seedlings attracts the dreaded carrot fly. The positive note is that seedlings are actually as delicious as the main crop. The leaves are so tasty.

I prefer to broadcast sow my carrots in a haphazard way rather than drill sowing in straight lines. It rather depends on the kind of crop you want to grow. Broadcast sowing produces a good crop of smaller roots, mainly because the plants are closer together and have to compete for light, water and nutrients. Sowing in rows allows roots to develop because you thin them out to allow plenty of room between the plants. Sowing in drills also allows you to hoe cleanly down the rows. But, with limited time on my hands, I went for broadcast and had terrific crops of tasty roots.

I particularly liked the variety Parmex because it matured quickly, the skins were smooth, making cleaning them at the plot easy, and the roots were just a bit smaller than a golf ball and so sweet. I bet they would grow well in containers. Autumn King (I think it was actually Autumn King 2) produces more traditional-shaped carrots, which were quite heavy and apparently they can be left in the ground without any danger of splitting. Mine were never in danger of splitting because we ate them all before I needed to store or leave any for later. I also grew Flyaway and, as the name and blurb promised, the carrot fly did stay away.

···⟩
SOWING CARROTS
1 Carrot seeds are tiny. They can be mixed with a handful or two of fine sand to help even sowing. **2** Broadcast them as evenly as possible across finely tilthed soil and lightly rake. **3** Make sure to label them with the date that you sowed them. **4** Always water seeds in with a rose on the watering can.

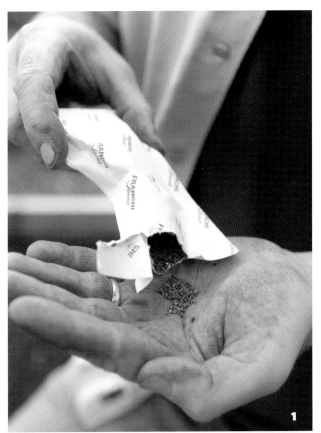

CLIMBING FRENCH BEANS

I do like my French beans (and I deplore runner beans – apologies to all you allotmenteers who think every plot should have a wigwam or two of them. There are so many of the things around that growers cannot give them away – and I just don't like their taste). Anyway, it's a different matter with my French beans; they are gorgeous, especially when eaten young and uncooked from the plant and, if we ever get one, survive better in hot, dry summers than runners.

Climbing French beans reach around two metres (6 foot) high, so they definitely need some sort of structure to climb up. I made an avenue of canes, all securely fastened with cable ties. I prepared the soil to a magic recipe (see page 186) another plot holder had told me about. I actually did the work in spring, but ideally it is best done in winter. It really produced great results, improved the soil no end, and I was delighted to find every seed germinated.

I planted the seeds directly into this well-prepared soil, one seed per hole, with two holes at the base of each cane. The trick when sowing directly into the soil is to wait until the soil has warmed up (a good indication is when annual weed seeds start to grow) and to time the sowing of your beans to make sure that when they emerge into the light the frost isn't going to nab them. Just in case a wayward snail or slug has a go at your seedlings, sow a few extra at the end of the row to act as spares. Another good tip is to sow the seeds on the inside of the cane structure. That makes sure that when you are vigorously hoeing around you don't accidentally nick the seedlings or, later on, the plants.

I grew a couple of varieties and fancy trying a couple more next year. Cobra was a terrific bean that produced hundreds of pods from my 20 or so plants. These plants either loved my soil or are the best variety to grow for yield. Or, you never know, maybe both. Pods will get to around 15 cm long or so, but I do like to pick them young. They taste delicious and not too beany, if you know what I mean. Subtle might be the word to describe them.

My other variety was one that Keith had saved from the previous year but had forgotten the name. I know, not much help, but a good example of how your allotment neighbours will offer seeds and advice. Next year I fancy growing the variety St Anna for a larger, juicer pod (I'm really getting the taste for beans) and Sultana promises pencil-shaped pods on tall plants, each pod packed with flavour. Looking into it, I might grow some Trionfo Violetta. The pods are purple and turn green when cooked. They will look great on the plot.

···⦂

CONSTRUCTING A CLIMBING BEAN FRAME
1 Prepare the soil (see p 186) and rake it so that it is level. Start with the ends of the frame. Push two canes into the ground approximately 60 cm apart, at either end of your trench. Tie the end canes at the top. **2** Place a cross cane across the top to add some support. **3** Evenly space canes approximately 30 cm (12 inches) apart along the length of the trench. Do the same on the other side so that the canes are opposite each other. **4** Once they are in place, push the canes into the ground. Tie each pair of canes to the cross cane at the top to create a strong structure.

SALAD LEAVES

This is one of the most useful crops you will grow. The bagged stuff from supermarkets tends to go off quickly, and some is washed in water that's saturated in chlorine. Growing your own produces top-quality leaves that can be eaten minutes after picking without, if you choose, any artificial additives or flavourings.

The key to self-sufficiency in salad is to sow a few seeds every fortnight, this way you don't get too much all at once. You can sow these outdoors at this time, but I actually grew a few containers of salad leaves at home, and also put some seeds into small individual pots which I transplanted into the allotment.

I went for the cheapest option and bought a few packets of mixed salad leaf seeds. I did sow them too thickly at first, but soon got the hang of sowing thinly. That's the great thing about successional sowing, you quickly learn from your mistakes and soon get a chance to put your new-found skills into practice. So, it's a pinch of seed onto the surface of your compost. Don't, whatever you do, cover the seeds with a thick layer of compost; a thin layer of vermiculite will suffice.

SOWING SALAD LEAVES
1 Salad leaves can be sown directly onto the top surface of the soil or compost. Sow as thinly as possible. I use a board to keep me off the soil. **2** Cover with a very thin layer of soil, or you can use some compost or vermiculite, which will help you delineate the line better. **3** Make sure to always label your plants with the date you sow them. Writing on the packet and putting a stick through it is ideal.

POTATOES

Around mid-spring I put in all my potatoes on the same day, as Peter had advised. You can put the chitted earlies in earlier, but I had missed the boat so instead I planted them all at the same time with a view to harvesting them at different times from early summer on, again, on Peter's advice, as he said that was the way he did it.

I had seven different varieties in total; it sounds like a lot, but we do like our potatoes and I did think that I could always give some away if need be. Swift were, and always will be, the first to go in during a ceremonial planting. The great thing about potatoes is that they are ideal for new, unworked ground: you dig a trench to put them in, you earth them up (which involves more breaking up of the soil) and then, of course, you dig again when harvesting. As a result, the soil where my potatoes were is now some of the best soil on the entire plot. If I rotate where I put them in over a few years, all the soil will be well worked.

GLOBE ARTICHOKES

The ones Keith gave me didn't have the best of starts, but they pulled through. They lay on the soil all day under the baking (okay, warm) sun and in the drying wind. When filming finished I planted them and watered them with a couple of gallons per plant. They flagged, they sulked for a week, but then they picked up. They really proved to be the most resilient of plants. All survived and, planted 30 cm (12 inches) apart, formed a solid wall in no time. Although I didn't have a crop this year, I should have one or two buds to pick next year and then I'll be lifting and splitting them and giving them away to any other newcomers to the site.

JERUSALEM ARTICHOKES

I did everything right, but they never came. I planted the knobbly tubers into a lovely trench containing a thick mattress of council compost and topped with a duvet of the same – similar to how I planted the potatoes. It was salt in the wound when the *Gardeners' World* garden at Berryfields produced a wall of leaf, flower and roots in late summer. I'll definitely try again next year.

PEAS

I love a good pea (stop it), and they seem to grow on everyone's plot on the site. I sowed all the seeds directly into the soil and wasn't too concerned about the weather as these seedlings are tough. It is, however, crucial not to put the seeds into cold, wet soil – if you do so, they will rot.

Depending on the type of spring we have they germinate pretty quickly; I planted them in mid-April and the seedlings were up within a fortnight. If you have problems with pigeons, it is worth netting your seedlings. Mice also get stuck into them. A plot holder told me to put cut holly branches along the row to deter both. I did this, didn't put any netting up and all the seedlings came through unscathed.

I prepared the soil as I did for my French beans, supported the growing plants with bamboo canes secured with cable ties, and they did well. However there was a mottling on the leaves of one of the varieties. Royal Horticultural Society staff reckoned it was a virus problem and could even have come in on the seeds from the outset. Pea mosaic virus is carried on the seed, but to be honest it could have been a dry spell and the copious amounts of water I drenched them with. I was using the dip tank on the plot as opposed to rainwater, which can cause similar symptoms because it's easily contaminated (albeit accidentally) by other plotholders. Whatever caused the virus, the plants completely switched off in mid-summer, but fortunately it was after I'd harvested bucket-loads of pods.

I tried Purple Podded, where for a change the name does a great job, and Ne Plus Ultra, an old variety dating back to the 1800s that produces long, straight pods of superb-tasting peas.

SOWING PEAS

1 I prefer using cable ties for wigwams as they are easier and stronger than string and can be re-used. I've used four 1.8 metre (6 foot) long bamboo poles, pushed into the ground. **2** Make two holes about 5 centimetres (2 inches) deep with a dibber or your finger and drop a pea into the bottom. Add an extra one as insurance; if they both come up the weaker one can be removed. **3** Cover over the soil with your hand and water in well. Be sure to keep your peas well watered throughout the growing season.

COMPANION PLANTING

Companion planting is a vicious game of hide and seek, allied forces and decoy planting all rolled into one. The only rule of engagement is that monocultures, or plots stuffed with one type of plant, are a thing of the past. Sure, there's safety in numbers but also longevity with diversity.

Insects, the pesky kinds, home in on your crops by looking at them, smelling them or feeling them. A cabbage white butterfly can spot a ripe brassica leaf from hundreds of metres away. So, mix up brassica and carrots, throw in a few herbs and maybe a large leaved pumpkin or two and it's as good as making them invisible.

Well, that's the theory. Put simplistically, companion planting is all about choosing plants that have additional properties and functions beyond simply being ornamental or edible when used in combination with one another. And you thought growing your own veg was simple!

But what grows best with what? If you have ever grown carrots then you know about carrot fly. Likewise, if you know your onions then you are an expert on onion fly. Both flies are attracted to their hosts by smell. That's why you are always reading about why you shouldn't thin your carrots on a breezy afternoon. Ideally you shouldn't thin them at all as any smell in the air can be picked up by the fly. It therefore makes perfect sense to grow carrots and onions together. The smell of the carrots is masked by the onions, and would you believe it, the smell of the onions is masked by the carrots.

There are other ways in which companion planting benefits your crops:

- Large plants can shelter others, such as planting a hedge to break damaging winds.
- Leafy plants provide shade for plants that need it, and can also retain moisture in the soil.
- I planted fennel at the ends of my brassica rows. The idea is that when one runs to seed, the smell attracts parasitic wasps, which in turn feed on caterpillars on the brassicas.
- Plant nasturtiums around the plot and a whole host of problems are solved. If you put nasturtiums near your cabbages the strong smell of the nasturtium leaves will act as a magnet for caterpillars, resulting in clean, healthy cabbages growing unhindered. Nasturtiums will also lure woolly aphids away from your apple trees and attract blackfly from nearly anything. And let's face it, nasturtiums don't ask for much in return. They'll grow in any soil, in most conditions and all without additional watering in dry periods, nor feed in hungry spells. In a good year they will grow like wildfire and flower themselves silly.

I haven't tried this lot but fellow plotholders have mentioned them to me:

- Asparagus prevents nematodes from attacking tomato roots.
- Tansy stops ants in their tracks.
- Chives deter aphids from landing on your tomatoes and cucumbers.
- Chervil keeps aphids away from your lettuce.
- Coriander grown near anything will stop aphid attacks.

1 Growing a few flowers alongside cabbages will help to mask their distinctive smell and hide them from pests such as the cabbage white butterfly.

2 Mexican marigolds not only look bright and cheery on the allotment, they are also a great companion plant and can be seen here alongside tomatoes.

The roots of the Mexican marigold, an annual which grows to about 1.2 metres (4 feet), have an insecticidal effect on nematodes and some effect on keeled slugs. The roots secrete a chemical about 3 months after sowing and this can also affect the growth of ground elder, bindweed, couch grass and ground ivy. Anything that keeps keeled slugs off potatoes has to be worth a try.

In addition to companion planting there are other ways in which we can use plants to help us out on the allotment:

Good old-fashioned survival of the fittest comes into play. Some plants can smother others making the garden a better place to be. For example, tagetes planted in number can smother bindweed.

Problems with mice? Then plant some elder. The rodents are put off by the smell.

Increased plant diversity = more wildlife = more pest predators – which is no bad thing. Supply dense undergrowth near your plot, and toads, frogs, hedgehogs and nesting birds will be more disposed to take up residence, much to the annoyance of slugs, snails, aphids and other insect pests.

Planting up young plants

As spring moved into summer, the temperatures of the soil and sun rose, and all risk of frost had passed, so it was safe to plant out yet more crops and really fill up my plot. I planted out all of these as plants, bulbs or tubers, rather than seeds, which meant they could go in a bit later but would still produce a crop this season.

BRASSICAS

I did buy a few plants in to supplement my home-raised seedlings. When buying in brassica seedlings, make sure they don't look like they have been hanging about in the shop for a long time. If the garden centre forgets to water them, allows them to wilt and then drenches them, the plants will pick up but run the risk of bolting or running to seed and never producing a crop later in the year.

Things to look for are wilted plants or plants with yellow lower leaves. Don't buy them. If the variety isn't red, as in red cabbage, avoid buying any seedlings with reddish leaves or anything with a blue tinge to the leaves. Chances are they have been chilled and, again, bolting is a real risk later in the year. The trick with all brassicas is to keep them growing and never allow them to have a check in growth. This could be caused by a couple

1 Young brassica plants like these brussel sprouts always need covering up to keep the birds off. 2 Some really healthy looking pot grown plants just waiting to go into the ground.

of cold nights, plunging them from your windowsill straight outside
or allowing them to dry out.

A fellow plot holder told me that the best way to avoid any problems
with root diseases and to get plants off to a flying start is to plant them
in specially prepared planting holes filled with a particular compost mix.
The idea being that the roots romp into the mix before anything nasty
can attack the roots. It worked.

This is his magic recipe:
- A bucket of compost (council stuff in my case, or home-made if you have it)
- Quarter of a bucket of grit
- A handful of fish, blood and bone, or any general fertilizer you use
- A handful of crushed eggshells
- A dusting of garden lime

I also discovered from the die-hard allotmenteers that there are other
tips and tricks for getting a good crop when planting:
- Plant deep: ignore the little seedling leaves and plant up to the lower
pair of proper leaves.
- Plant hard: firm the soil around the plants to prevent the top-heavy plants
from rocking around and damaging stems.
- Plant wet: water the mix before you plant and again after planting. This
settles the soil around the roots and minimizes the chance of shocking the
plants into stopping growing. If they stop growing they run to seed later on.

Then, finish off with two more tricks to stop airborne attacks:
- A cardboard collar, 15 cm (6 inches) square, with a slit cut into it is placed
around the base of the stems to stop attack from cabbage root fly. Cabbage
root flies lay eggs near the base of plants that hatch and the resultant
maggots follow the stem down to the roots where they cause havoc. The
collar stops the maggots getting down, with many eggs drying out on the
cardboard before they even develop into maggots.
- Netting: as everyone tells me on every site around the country, 'If you don't
net it, you don't get it'.

At first I thought the amount of faffing around wasn't worth it for a couple
of caulis and maybe a cabbage, but once you have tasted home-grown
brassicas you will go to any length to ensure success; they have to be one
of the tastiest crops you can produce.

JOE'S BRASSICA PLANTING MIX

1 I always mix up a full barrow of this stuff, which makes enough for a generous helping for 6–8 plants. It all starts with a barrowful of garden compost, and plenty of grit or sharp sand. **2** Chuck in a couple of handfuls of lime, especially for neutral to acid soils, to help deter club root. **3** Add 3 or 4 handfuls of an organic fertiliser to feed the plants. I use fish, blood and bone. **4** Mix it all together thoroughly in the barrow and pick out any twigs. **5** Dig a decent hole about a spade's width all round and a spit deep for each plant. Pour in some of your prepared compost. **6** Crumble an eggshell into each hole and mix it up with the compost. Brassicas love a bit of calcium to start them off. **7** Firm the compost down hard using your fist or even your feet so it's fairly solid. **8** Pop out each plant from its pot. It's best

to soak plants for at least a few hours or even overnight before planting them out. **9** Plant each plant deeper than it is in the pot and really firm in well around it. They can even be planted to their bottom leaves to give them extra support. **10** Water each plant thoroughly; I use at least half a large watering can for each one. **11** Make your own brassica collar by cutting a piece of cardboard into a square with a small circle in the middle. Cut a slit from one edge to the centre and carefully place around the base of the plant, twisting the card at the slit so that it wraps around the stem. This provides a preventative barrier against root fly. **12** Yup, as you should know by now, if you don't net it, you don't get it, so make sure to cover your plants carefully with netting right down to soil level.

ONIONS

Whenever you visit allotment sites, I guarantee you will see entire plots planted up with onions. All I will say is that the plot holders must love them, as most sites have a 'produce cannot be sold' rule in their handbook.

Onions are a delight to grow. The two main ways to grow them is by seed and by set. I grew mine from sets, which are specially prepared little onions. They are in suspended animation, and when they come into contact with moisture and warmth, they start to grow. One set equals one bigger onion.

The best time to plant most of your maincrop onions is March and April. The soil is warming up and there's usually a lot of moisture around. However, if your soil is cold or you just don't get round to it (and sets can start growing in the nets they arrive in) you can plant them into small cells or individually into pots. Keep them in a cold frame or cold greenhouse and plant out into the soil when you, or it, are ready. The added benefit of doing this is that the plants are actively growing so there is no chance of them rotting in the soil. You always get a couple of dud onion sets in any batch, and there is nothing more annoying than finding out which ones they are by the no-shows in your row of plants.

The actual planting is easy. Use a trowel to dig out a small hole and drop the set in up to its neck. Push the soil back around the set, and there you go. Space them about 20 cm (8 inches) apart to allow for development and good air circulation around the plants. If you have preplanted them in pots of multipurpose compost, simply transplant them as you would any other plant – dig a hole, carefully knock the plant and as much rootball as possible out of the pot, put into the soil, firm around, and water.

It's always worth checking your newly-planted sets because birds like to pull at the strawy, worm-like parts above the soil. If any are pulled out, plant them back again. Avoid pushing sets into the soil, though, as this can cause a hard pan of soil beneath the set, and when the emerging roots hit the pan they actually push the whole set out of the soil. If this happens, replant using a trowel.

I planted a few varieties including Turbo, which is a lovely round onion that stores well into winter; Sturon, which is a no-nonsense onion producing medium-sized, mild and juicy bulbs and also the delicious, strong-tasting red onion Red Baron, which produced a heavy crop. I love the colour of the sets; it's a deep crimson, which gives a red rim to each ring when sliced. Other onions, such as the Japanese onions and some later-planting varieties such as Radar, should ideally be planted in the autumn along with garlic, but I missed them in my first year.

···⟩
Onions can be grown from seed, but sets are readily available, easy to handle and more reliable. Squeeze each one before planting to check it's not soft or rotten.

POTATOES

Potatoes seem to be a big thing on allotments. Everyone grows some and everyone has their own way of going about it. Some chit (I'll get back to that), some earth up (and that), some use spare potatoes from the supermarkets (definitely that) and others swear by particular varieties (I'll add to that).

I did it this way: I bought certified virus-free stock from a mail order company. Why? Because I didn't want to run the risk of planting anything that was riddled with a virus – a virus I wouldn't see the effects of until it was too late and the plants were growing. The potatoes you buy from supermarkets, or even saved ones from last year's crop, may have potato viruses present, which could affect the crop later on. It's an insurance policy, but it's good veg-growing practice.

I chitted my seed potatoes in about February, once I'd got them. All this means is to get them into growth before planting out. To do this, simply put the seed potatoes into a few trays and egg boxes with the ends with the most eyes (little growing buds) uppermost and put them in a cool, light place. This will encourage the shoots to develop. Ideally the potatoes will produce shoots about 4 cm (1.5 inches) long that are solid, stubby and either green or reddish pink.

Planting out is a case of timing. The idea is that by the time the shoots have developed and are well and truly on their way, all danger of frost should have passed. What I did was to dig a trench 10 cm (4 inches) or so deep and the width of a spade. I put a layer of compost in the base and nuzzled my chitted potatoes about 25 cm (10 inches) apart along the trench. I then filled the trench with the removed soil and mounded it up by another 5 cm (2 inches). It looked great and really professional.

I got a little bit worried when I saw Keith putting his potatoes into flat soil with a bulb planter, but I stuck with what I thought was right. Sure enough, the shoots appeared and I started the process of earthing up. All you do (or what I did), is ease some soil up and around the developing shoots. This does two things: it protects any developing potatoes from being exposed to the sun (where they turn green and are potentially poisonous), and encourages more stem growth, which helps to increase the weight of the crop. You do this every now and again as needed until you have 20 cm (8 inches) of earthed up stem, then you let the shoots develop. For the record, Keith's spuds did really well, which proves that there is more than one way to plant a spud.

Harvesting is another milestone in your allotment year. Competitive allotmenteers can't wait to claim the first 'new' potatoes of the year.

You can join in with this race or wait until your early varieties start to flower, which is often a sign that they are ready for harvesting. When your maincrop varieties flower, however, leave them a little longer until the foliage turns an off-green colour, then you can start digging in. Some people leave their plants and crops in the soil until they need them, digging as they require, but if you do this you run the risk of losing them to slugs. I'd dig them up from October onwards and store them in potato sacks in a cool, dark place to prevent them sprouting.

There are lots of varieties to choose from. Mail order offers more of a selection, but garden centres sell the favourite, tried-and-tested varieties. There is one I just couldn't resist…

One of the earliest of earlies, is Swift. It's great for growing in pots and containers as the foliage is shorter than most and it has good disease resistance. It was the first potato I grew and you might have seen me cooking the very first spuds and eating them on camera. They took me a step closer to heaven – and if you've ever grown your own spuds, you'll know what I mean.

Charlotte is a great early variety for the first-time allotmenteer as it is reliable and has a great flavour. If you want to chance it with the slugs, you can also leave them in the ground to get larger. Duke of York is a quality, old early variety with pale yellow, waxy flesh. I loved the taste. Lady Christl

SOWING SEED POTATOES
1 Planting potatoes is a doddle. Dig a trench about 10–15 cm (4–6 inches) deep and dig in some compost. Nuzzle each potato into the bottom, about 25 cm (10 inches) apart.
2 Incorporate some more compost into the loose soil and backfill the trench. Potatoes are perfect as a first crop on new ground because they help to break up new, unworked soil.

is another early variety with good flavour and a heavy crop of waxy tubers.

Onto the maincrops, and I planted out a new variety called Mayan Gold. It was bred from one of the original potato species and was given to me by my good mate Cleve West on one of his visits to the plot. It was one of the earliest maincrops to be harvested; the yield was good and each tuber was quite small. Another variety, Pentland Dell, worried me for a time because of its naturally scraggy foliage. However, the crops were good and many of the tubers were large enough to use as baking potatoes. The taste is definitely there. (Apparently this is the one that frozen chip companies use.)

I also thought I'd play it safe and try a few blight resistant varieties (see page 137). Sarpo Axona and Sarpo Mira are both later maincrop varieties and both produced medium-sized crops of floury spuds with an earthy taste. After speaking with a plot holder in Scotland, I realised I should have cut the haulms or stems off the plants in September and just let the potatoes sit in the soil. Apparently this stops their development and prevents them turning too starchy. Maybe that was the earthy taste I was picking up. I have to say, they weren't touched by blight and the slugs also left them well alone. Rumour has it that Sarpo Mira is also drought-resistant, but this was hard for me to prove as drought wasn't a problem last year!

···⋗
I may have bought this sieve for my soil, but it works just as well for draining the freshest spuds I've ever tasted.

⋮⋮
Once we started harvesting our earlies, they just kept coming and coming. We didn't have to buy any more spuds for the whole year.

Looks pretty good eh? Well they were by far the tastiest sweetcorn I've ever had. Some allotment holders have a pan of water ready boiled before they pick them and swear that's the way to do it. I took mine straight home to the kids.

SOWING SWEETCORN

1 These plastic cells are perfect for starting off many plants, including sweetcorn. Fill the tray with compost and make a hole in one of the modules with a dibber. **2** Drop a corn seed in and lightly cover with more compost. **3** Water well, keep frost free and plant out once they've grown into strong little plants.

SWEETCORN

The whole family loves sweetcorn, so I promised to grow as many plants as I could. I was a little disappointed when I found out that each plant would only produce three cobs, four if I was lucky, but, undeterred, I planted up some plants I'd raised from seed as a late spring crop.

I was told to plant them quite deep and then, once they got growing, to mound the soil up around their stems to increase stability and encourage roots to grow from the base of the stems. I also followed the traditional advice of planting in blocks, as opposed to rows. The thinking is that the pollen from the male flower, produced at the top of the plant, is blown into the block where the female flowers are forming lower down on the plants. If the plants were in a row, I suppose the risk of pollen blowing away (and onto someone else's plants) is higher.

Again, it all worked well. They're a really good looking plant too, adding height without too much spread. You can tell when they're ripe by pulling the leaves back and squeezing a kernel. If milky juice comes out, they're ready. I can't describe the difference in flavour between shop-bought and home-grown sweetcorn. Home-grown wins every time. I grew Supersweet which, as the name implies, is sweeter than most, and I intend to go sweetcorntastic next year, sowing them in succession to keep them coming.

A PLANT CALLED COMFREY

I got some stick about how I pronounced the name of this plant. Comfrey or cumfrey? It doesn't matter to me because I do know that it is a real organic allotment plant, and once I had planted a couple of rows I really felt like I'd arrived on the allotment scene.

Symphytum x uplandium (easier to get right than comfrey or cumfrey) is a special plant and the best variety to get is one called Bocking 14. It's sterile so it won't produce seeds that will germinate all over your plot. It does, however, spread and thicken up and will produce great patches of invaluable foliage. I made the mistake of thinking two rows would stay neat and tidy, and planted root sections straight across the biggest of the triangular beds on the plot. I can tell you that all this stuff wants to do is grow. The neat and tidy rows, 60 cm (24 inches) apart, soon merged and produced a small thicket. It needed to be moved and I reckon it is an ideal plant to bung into an unwanted corner of the plot. So that's what I did. It is tolerant of sun, partial shade and near deep shade. Damp soil is best so it will thrive near the ever-leaking water tank on the corner of my plot. Once you have it you've got it for a long time; if you dig it up and leave any piece of root in the soil it will grow into a new plant.

But what's the big deal with comfrey? I kind of knew instinctively that an allotment needed a few plants of it, but when other plot holders told me what it could be used for I was amazed.

It is simply the best stuff to add loads of nutrients to a compost heap. The roots go down deep and drag up nutrients, especially potassium, and this ends up in the leaves of the plant. When you put the leaves on the compost heap they rot down and release the nutrients into the mix.

Still in the compost heap, comfrey leaves actually speed up the rotting process. That's because the richness of the leaves – and it's a natural richness – encourages the bacterial and fungal activity to move on quickly.

You can line potato trenches with a layer of its leaves in spring. The leaves will rot down and provide essential nutrients for the developing spuds. Because comfrey grows so quickly I decided to use chopped leaves as mulch around my potatoes later on in the year. This will provide essential water retention and again will release nutrients around the plants.

Comfrey leaves can be soaked in water to create a fantastic liquid feed. Now I know gardening isn't an exact science, and running an allotment is even further from any text book you care to imagine, but making comfrey feed has to be my kind of chemistry. Fill an old dustbin or bucket a quarter full with leaves, top up with water, cover (and this is advisable – trust me, this stuff stinks to high heaven as it rots) and wait four weeks. Then all you have to do is to dip in your watering can and water your plants. It's particularly effective with tomatoes and runner beans (so I'm told). You can make a concentrated version of this magic juice so that you can store it for use whenever you want. Simply stuff some leaves into a container with no added water and put a weight such as a paving slab or stone on top.

···>
MAKING COMFREY FEED

1 Fill up an old dustbin or bucket with water. 2 Harvest the comfrey from your plants by cutting the leaves back to the ground. A couple of large handfuls will do – they'll grow back quickly. 3 Rip or chop the leaves up and drop them into the water. 4 Give it a good stir at the start and let it stew for four weeks, stirring occasionally. Top up with water if it dries out during hot weather. You'll know it's ready because it really stinks.

The resultant brown juice can be drained thought a small hole made in the base of the container. I've seen this work well when comfrey leaves have been stuffed into a length of drainpipe and a piece of mesh fixed over the base. Store the juice in bottles and use within the year, diluting one part comfrey juice with 15 parts water.

This is for my plot neighbour, Keith. You can feed wilted comfrey leaves to chickens. It's a great addition to their all-round diet. The leaves are low in carbohydrate and high in protein and this is the mix your average chicken likes. But, chickens? Maybe next year.

Seasonal problems

In spring things move extremely quickly on the allotment. It needs a regular input of focused energy, and if you're not careful it will get on top of you and ultimately beat you. Even in my relatively short spell as an allotmenteer I've seen plot holders come and go at this time of year.

We had a very warm April, so everything started growing at an alarming rate. Of course it was good to see what I had put in taking off and putting on growth, but it was spring when the horsetail decided to pay me back big time for chopping it up into thousands of pieces. Although I thoroughly weeded over areas before planting, it was impossible to get every bit out of the ground. Some days I'd turn up to sow something new or prepare an area, and all I could see was a sea of little green shoots all over the plot. Picking through it between larger plants such as the potatoes, calabrese, raspberry canes, etc, wasn't too bad, but it's an absolute nightmare when it gets in between the garlic and shallots and comes up between young seedlings, as in those situations it is extra fiddly and time consuming to get out. Cathy would come up with the kids and spend hours just picking through it. At first it really wound her up, but I think she found it quite therapeutic after a while.

We had put in some broad bean plants and they quickly got infested with blackfly. This seemed to be a common problem with other plot holders too, and although I sprayed an organic soft soap solution it was too late for them. A bigger frustration was the Jerusalem artichokes that Cleve had given me. I waited and waited for them to come up, but they just never showed. They are meant to be unbelievably tough and resilient, and other allotmenteers have told me that they can't get rid of theirs and have to mow them over with a lawnmower to stop them! I dug one up to find the reason why they never showed. It had been eaten by slugs and was now rotten through. I really wanted to grow them to eat, as they're one of my favourites, but visually I wanted them to help create some height too as they have tall, sunflower-like flowers. I'll just have to try again next year.

Birds are a real problem on our site. They are particularly fond of brassicas, especially in winter when their other food sources are scarce. Fortunately Keith suggested that I net my brassicas as soon as I planted them, and it certainly worked.

My goji berries have also been a running saga. I've tried tasting dried goji berries and heard that fresh ones are particularly delicious and nutritious, so I thought they'd be something different to grow, and I'd also heard that they were extremely tough bushes. Foolproof, I thought.

Well, I bought some bare-rooted plants by mail order, from a reputable supplier, and Cathy planted them. That programme went out and pretty much immediately a viewer contacted the BBC message board to let us know that there was a problem with plants that originated from the Far East and it was worth checking it out in detail with DEFRA.

Well, to cut a long story short, it turned out that goji berry plants can carry a disease which could have wiped out everybody's potatoes and tomatoes (as they are all in the same family). I didn't want that responsibility on my shoulders, so I dug them up, sealed them in a bin liner and put them in with my household rubbish immediately. The Goji berries were subsequently known as the 'No Go Joe' berries!

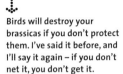

Birds will destroy your brassicas if you don't protect them. I've said it before, and I'll say it again – if you don't net it, you don't get it.

Carrots and their flies

My kids love raw carrots. As a fly, carrot root fly also loves carrots, as its name suggests. The battle of the plot continues.

The children grew fast-growing, round carrots by sowing them early and, yes, they were rewarded with decent crops. That's because they grew and were harvested before the dreaded carrot fly got cracking. It first appears in late April and May when it flies close to the ground, laying eggs at the base of carrot leaves. These eggs hatch, usually within a week, and the grubs burrow down, feeding on the roots of your developing carrots.

The first signs of attack are yellowing and reddening of leaves, which, if mine were anything to go by, look sickly. That's the only way to describe it. You instinctively know that something is wrong, and then when you pull up the plants you'll see networks of tunnels caused by the hungry grubs, and the creamy white beasts themselves. It is so sad as the plants will have been growing for weeks and you get nothing at the end. Once the initial spring swarm has gone, you can expect another generation to attack in late July.

The actual fly, with its reddish-brown head on a body 8 mm (0.3 inches) long, is hard to spot; and even then all you can do is shoo it away. There are ways and means of avoiding trouble, though. The best solution is to avoid attracting it in the first place. Carrot flies detect your carrots by smell. When you thin your carrot seedlings the flies can pick up the smell up to a couple of miles away, or even further if you thin your seedlings on a breezy day. If you have to thin, do it on a still or rainy day. The smell stays within your plot and you reduce the risk of fly attack. But from experience I know it is difficult to sow so thinly that you don't need to hoick a few out.

There are varieties of carrots that are resistant to carrot fly. These have been specially bred to contain less chlorogenic acid, a naturally-occurring chemical that the grubs need to survive. Therefore, the less chlorogenic acid is in the root, the less chance the grubs have of surviving. Brilliant. I grew one of these varieties, Flyaway, and it came through unscathed.

I was told by a number of plot holders that all that's needed to keep carrot fly away is a barrier 45 cm (18 inches) high around the crop. Apparently, carrot flies don't fly very high and when they come up against this Great Wall of China they perish. I put up a barrier, but surely the flies get blown around in the breeze and can drop anywhere? If your carrots have been attacked don't leave them in the ground and be thorough in your autumn clean up. Once you have removed the roots, give the area a good dig to expose the larvae to the elements and birds.

····⟩
**HOW TO CONSTRUCT
A CARROT FLY BARRIER**
1 Push in some canes around the carrots, leaving one cane loose. **2** Wrap the end of a length of fleece around the loose cane and tie it in (again my trusty cable ties do the job nicely and can easily be pushed through the fleece). Push the cane into the soil. **3** Wrap the length of the fleece around all the canes until you've come full circle, making sure not to leave any gaps, and tie it in. **4** Plastic bottles help to keep the fleece taught and protect your eyes when you're bending down.

Horsetail – the bad news

I've already explained why I cultivated the plot knowing there was horsetail present, but I have to go a little bit deeper into what this dreadful plant is like. I say dreadful, but boy, is it a survivor or what? My plot is infested with field horsetail, or *Equisetum arvense*. It is a prehistoric plant and has been around in one form or another for millions of years. Guess I'm up against it really.

The main way it spreads is by the tough, stringy rhizomes that Keith, my neighbour, has been earnestly sieving out for two years now. Someone with a lot of time on his hands has discovered that a 10 cm (4 inch) long piece of rhizome will produce 64 metres (70 yards) of growth in a year. That same person also calculated that a lone piece of rhizome would infest an area the size of Lord's Cricket Ground in six years. Howzat for persistence? It's a monster.

So, these rhizomes mean business. New plants will grow from any section left in the soil, making a little light weeding purely cosmetic, as I found out. I'm not kidding when I tell you I weeded a bed, turned around and new shoots had sprung up almost immediately. They also produce structures with spores that can result in new plants – not so many this way, but yet more to add to the mix. The spore-producing structures appear in April and the vegetative stems in late April and May. On my plot, most growth happened in July when the plant went berserk. And while all this top growth was causing concern (or mirth) to some viewers, those dastardly rhizomes were burrowing up to 3 metres (10 feet) down into the soil.

Did I mention they also produce little tuberous energy stores just in case things get tough? Well, they do on most nodes or places where the rhizome splits. They can persist in the soil for years waiting for the conditions to be right for growth.

Am I painting a dark picture of allotment life? Horsetail can put you off gardening for good, but it won't beat me and I will persist in taking the tops off, digging up and removing as many of the rhizome pieces I can. Every time I visit I vow to take away at least a bucket full of rhizomes. It's the only way. I could spray, but quite honestly that is a last resort. I could cover areas not under cultivation with cardboard or black plastic and hope to smother the plants. The top growth will die but the rhizomes will sit there waiting. Also, there's very little of my plot that isn't under cultivation.

If you are starting out and choosing a plot I would ask your allotment officer or site secretary whether or not horsetail is present and is it in your

····}
Even looking at pictures of this stuff turns me into Mister Angry. Just look at the rhizomes at the base. They're all broken off which means there's still plenty left in the ground.

proposed plot. Be direct, or forever – and sometimes it feels like it will be forever – be weeding. If you already have the dreaded horsetail then keep weeding and sieving. And in your darkest hour remember you are not alone.

Horsetail – the slightly better news

There is some good news, though. I was chatting to a biodynamic gardener who sympathized with my horsetail problem, but informed me there was a use for the shoots. She brews her own horsetail tea for use as a fungicide. To make this brew take 30 g/10 ounces of dried horsetails and simmer in an old pan containing 1.2 l/2 pints of rainwater for 30 minutes. (Make sure the pan isn't used for cooking, to avoid any chance of poisoning.) Leave it to stew for 24 hours and then dilute with more rainwater to make up 4.5 l/1 gallon. The mix should be a pale yellow colour. Give it a good old stir and store in a large container with a lid. This brew will last for a fortnight and can be directly sprayed onto plants to reduce the risk of mildew (my courgettes), blackspot (my roses at home) and rust (on some mint plants on the plot). Spray early in the season, every ten days.

Now I have to say I haven't used it yet, but it does endear me a little bit to the horsetail, as did finding out that the shoots can mop up cadmium, copper, lead and zinc, which can be toxic to plants and humans in high concentrations. The silica in the stems results in a rough, abrasive texture. There must be a use for that. Apparently horsetail can also accumulate gold in the stems. How come no one has told me of a simple recipe to extract that from the shoots? I've always said that the plot is a little gold mine.

Pots and containers can look great on the allotment and work like miniature raised beds in that they drain well and the soil warms up quickly inside in the spring. They can easily be covered if a light frost is forecast and are perfect for herbs and some quick-growing crops.

PLOT ESSENTIALS – SPRING
If you have one day a week at the plot make sure you:
- Get your seed packets in chronological order of sowing, not alphabetical.
- Warm up soil with cloches in case cold weather slows things down.
- Sort yourself out with a cold frame to harden off plants in before planting out.
- Keep on top of weeds while they're young – it's a good habit to get into.
- Be patient and check long-range weather forecasts. A lot of money and time can be lost due to unexpected frosts.
- Swap spare seeds with plot neighbours – there are usually too many for one person in a pack.

Joe's Veg Heroes
Peter Whiting

Peter Whiting won *Garden News'* Allotmenteer of the Year 2007. As you'd expect, his allotment, down in Bournemouth, is immaculate. Peter came and gave me plenty of encouragement, some good advice and a helping hand when I was starting my plot. Although he had never seen raised beds as diamonds and triangles like mine before, I think he liked them and helped me to put the framework together.

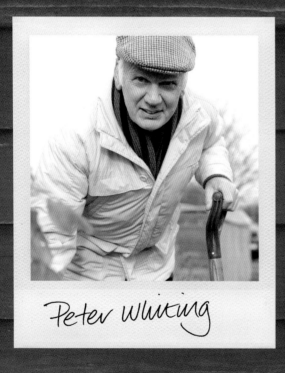

Peter Whiting

Allotment Longbarrow Allotments, Bournemouth, Dorset. The plot is approximately 450 square metres, i.e. 1 full-sized plot and one three-quarter-sized plot.

Annual rent £50 (a standard-sized plot is £30).

Soil type Light loam – perfect for veg growing if you add manure.

Biggest growing problem As a vegetable show exhibitor, a major problem at the moment is downy mildew on onions, and also blight on tomatoes and potatoes.

How much time do you spend on your plot? A couple of hours a day, weather permitting.

Favourite tool My Swoe, it just feels perfect in use and is just right for leaning on when 'nattering' with fellow plot holders. (A Swoe looks like a cross between a golf club and a hoe. The chamfered steel blade slides under the soil backwards and forwards, and can even be hooked around the back of a hard to reach plant. I couldn't live without mine – Joe.)

Favourite crop Dahlias really, but thinking of fruit and veg it would be difficult to single out any particular crop. I really do, however, look forward to the dinner that includes, for the first time in that year, new potatoes and mint, peas, carrots, beans, and anything else in season. Followed perhaps by strawberries.

Favourite time of year Late spring; because everything is green and bursting with growth.

What's your first memory of vegetable growing? My grandfather was a market gardener in East Anglia, and touring his huge garden – at least it seemed huge to me at the time – is one of my first ever memories.

When did you first grow vegetables? I had a small plot in my dad's garden from about the age of five.

How long have you had an allotment? I got my first allotment in 1976. It seemed the obvious thing to do at the time because we only had a small garden.

Why do you love growing fruit and vegetables so much? Freshness. I don't believe any shop can compete with the taste of my veg.

Why do you think growing your own is important? The exercise does me good, I know what has 'gone into them', and they simply taste better. I don't think, however, that you can use an economic argument.

What do you do with your excess produce? Give it away to friends and neighbours.

What is the best piece of growing advice you've been given? Get the soil in good condition, you can grow anything then (within reason).

What's the best advice you can give to other growers? Apart from the above advice, I tell new allotmenteers to make a plan of the layout they want (to avoid doing things more than once because they have put things in the wrong place); clear, properly, a small area of the plot and start growing the things they know they like; and then steadily extend the cleared areas, but don't try to do it all at once.

What would you do with your time if you didn't have an allotment? I can't imagine life without an allotment now. We have a plot holder on our site who is 94 and numerous 80-year-olds. I firmly believe their plots keep them not only physically active but mentally too. I fully intend to join them.

Summer at the plot

As spring moved into summer my allotment really started to look the business, and most of the ground was by now packed full of plants. More important than the aesthetics, however, was that it actually started producing enough food to keep us going for a full week, which felt like a significant achievement.

The first Swift new potatoes were lifted and ceremoniously cooked immediately outside the shed on a camping gas stove that Cathy and the kids bought me for my birthday. Now is it purely psychological that freshly dug, home-grown crops taste better than shop-bought, or is it that they just do? Well, whatever the answer, they tasted absolutely delicious and, apart from a few herbs and salads we'd had previously, were the first real produce that we had harvested.

The first year is certainly a slow burner, as it takes a while to get going. Some of the other plot holders, such as Ken, Keith and Manuel, were giving us what they couldn't eat themselves, which was really kind of them, and this kept us going and our spirits up. They were harvesting whatever they put in the autumn before, or had put in earlier than us that year, with the annual cycle all planned out and ticking over nicely.

The first year in particular feels like a lot of hard work and a very long wait before you really get a decent crop of anything. Once it starts coming, though, it just keeps coming – thick and fast! As well as the different varieties of potatoes we started to dig up, we were also harvesting lettuces, courgettes, peas, French beans, herbs, strawberries, and then squashes, cauliflowers, calabrese, sweet potatoes, raspberries, sweetcorn, tomatoes, chillies, fennel, garlic, onions, leeks and shallots, amongst others. Just listen to me rattling them all off; it makes me feel good listing them like that as I realise how much we'd achieved since February when the soil was cold, wet and impenetrable.

Of course, when the weather's warm you just want to be outside, and summer was when the allotment really became a focus for us getting together as a family. The long weekend days on the plot were just great and to go home late with our rewards made all the graft in the first half of the year feel worthwhile.

Summertime, and the living is easy ...

I quickly learnt that the summer soil is warm enough that any seeds sowed directly into it, such as rocket, coriander and mizuna, germinate quickly. I know everyone wants to get producing as quickly as possible, but I have found direct sowing far easier than faffing about with pots and trays at home and taking them to the allotment to transplant.

I know you're guaranteed a higher success rate with pots, because you only put in the strong plants that are growing on well and lose any failures, but you do still need to sow the seed and make sure the pots don't dry out on an almost daily basis. In the summer I get dragged all over the country filming and covering the RHS shows so, like many, I have to go for the easiest, least labour-intensive solution.

I also learnt that I like to broadcast seed whenever possible too, which meant scattering seed over a larger area and then thinning out the plants later when they get going. This worked particularly well with pak choi, carrots, and cut-and-come-again salad leaves.

With my first attempts I did get extremely frustrated at picking weeds out from between small seedlings, so I began to prepare those areas of soil particularly well before sowing any more. I bought a sieve and sieved out any weeds and stones in the top 15 cm/6 inches of soil and broke up the soil to a really fine tilth down to about the same depth. Although some of the horsetail still came through it, at least the seedlings were big enough to cope with me pulling the weeds out from between them, or I could lift out the small plants, weed and pop them straight back in.

My basil plants, I admit, were a pure cheat, but an undoubted success (see page 110). We had a cold wet spell for a while after planting and they just sat there sulking in the ground not doing much. When the weather did warm up they put on impressive strong growth, and nipping out the top buds encouraged them to bush out nicely. By mid-summer I was picking leaves on a regular basis, and by the end of the summer I had enough to make loads of pesto sauce. It's a trick I'll definitely be using again next year, as well as trying this technique out on some other herbs too. If there's an easy way, then I'm always up for trying it out.

There were still some areas on the plot that I simply didn't have time to tackle at all, such as the weed-filled patch around the compost heap and the shaded area under the tree. There was absolutely no way I could plant anything in these areas with my hands already full dealing with those I'd already cultivated, so I decided to cover them with whatever I could get my hands on to keep the weeds at bay. Old carpets are banned on my site, so I used old doors, old tarpaulins, cardboard and the old felt roof from the shed to cover the soil. This, I hoped, would kill off some of the weeds underneath, starving them of light and air, but I knew for sure that the horsetail would spring back the minute the barrier was lifted. Oh well, out of sight, out of mind was the idea!

I'm aware that long summer days are the good days on the allotment. Sure, the unpredictable weather could have been better in my first year, but in the summer the allotment becomes a fun, sociable place. Potato day summed it all up for me, as it really brought everyone together. It was all Sabina, another plotholder's idea as, to be frank, I didn't have a clue that it was the International Year of the Potato, specifically created to raise awareness that potatoes can be a food of the future and help relieve world poverty and starvation.

Plenty of people got involved on the day itself, and fortunately it was one of the hottest days of the summer. Everyone brought a dish (most with potatoes in them!), and there were lots of activities for the kids including, yup, you guessed it, hunt the potato. Gary, a plot holder who is also a professional juggler, put on a great act juggling with knives whilst walking blindfolded over someone lying on the ground. Rather him than me, that's for sure. I'd been practising my own allotment juggling all summer long, but for me that meant just trying to keep everything going on my plot!

What a scorcher! Potato Day was a great success and if we do anything like it again, I think I'll sell ice creams from my shed seeing as it's in a prime spot.

Summer crops

Summer really was a great time of year for me on my allotment; it had felt like everything up to now was weeding and containment, then early summer struck and all I was doing was sowing and planting. It felt positive. This was not the time just to sit back and enjoy the fruits of my labours. Nope, it was time to administer tender loving care to those crops that were maturing and nearing harvest, and also time to get another lot of crops going. Carrots, spring onions, a few late, late parsnips (I was busy weeding in March), endive and chicory. Next year's spring cabbage and leaf beet can both be sown at this time of year, too, so I put them in as well.

SWEET POTATOES

This is a vegetable I was unsure about. The textbooks told me they need a long, hot summer and plenty of moisture. The summer weather is obviously out of my hands, and as I'm not at the plot every day the plants could suffer during a dry spell. But I don't let things like that stop me.

The way to grow sweet potatoes is rather like dahlias. You buy little shoots, or slips, growing in March and April. These get potted up into multipurpose compost. Now, I did cheat a little bit here as I was helped by guys from the Royal Horticultural Society's garden at Hyde Hall in Essex. We filmed them potting up and putting sweet potatoes into a warm greenhouse prior to them, and me, planting out the rooted slips into well-prepared soil in the sunniest position on their site and my plot.

The fact that the plants need to be frost-free and planted into warm soil meant the slips didn't get out into the ground until June. Even then, it's best to warm the soil yourself by putting black plastic down for a month or so. This also encourages weak weed growth that can be removed before planting.

The actual planting is easy. Dig your hole, put in some compost and plant up to the level at which the slips are growing in the pot. Firm down, water well and stand back. Ideally, the soil should be free draining but capable of retaining water. In other words, forget it if your soil gets waterlogged, otherwise you should be okay.

I was then told two conflicting tales about my sweet potatoes. One was that they climbed and needed support, so I erected a wigwam of canes, just like you would for runner beans and peas. The other was that they sprawled in a bushy, slightly unruly manner. Mine did both, with the longest of the stems travelling up the canes with a little help and tying in.

The plants looked great. They are closely related to Morning Glory and the arrow-shaped leaves were mostly dark green. I could imagine growing them as lovely patio plants. Harvesting is interesting, as the plants need to be growing for about four months before anything gets formed. You can either harvest according to the calendar or wait until some of the leaves start to turn yellow. You can cook the green leaves and eat them as you would spinach, but it was the tubers I wanted.

Perceived knowledge is that you have to grow sweet potatoes in a polytunnel or a greenhouse to get any decent crop out of them. I tried a few varieties where the growers claimed a decent crop was obtainable without any protection. I grew Beauregard Improved, which has sweeter flesh that is also deeper orange than other varieties. It did okay in my clay soil in a cool, dark summer with me only visiting the plot once a week. Given a polytunnel, or at least a warm summer, it would romp away.

T65 is a more delicate-tasting sweet potato with yellowy flesh. It didn't crop as well as Beauregard Improved on my allotment, but the RHS had great success with it. In my opinion it is worth a go.

1 Some of the sweet potato varieties were happy to climb up wigwams with a little help, which saved me some ground space. **2** The produce may have been limited but they looked beautiful and tasted good too.

Herbs

We use a lot of herbs at home, so I decided to grow some of the culinary herbs we use most often.

BASIL

I took a bit of a flyer with growing basil on my plot. I love basil and we use a lot of it in our cooking, but it struck me that the price of seed was high, germination rates can be iffy, I was banned from putting any more seed trays indoors at home, and a greenhouse was still a dream.

Supermarkets, however, sell live basil in pots. There are a lot of seedlings crammed into the 1-litre pot, and early in spring they do look a little tatty, but that's because, just like the seedlings on windowsills around the country, each seedling is competing with its neighbours for light. But later in spring the plants seem healthier and well worth a gamble. I bought such a pot of basil for about a quid. On camera I gave the pot a good watering, knocked out the contents and divided up the clumps of seedlings into individual plants. I then planted these about 15 cm (6 inches) apart in each direction, watered them again and waited.

I got a few complaints, mainly from plant centres and herb specialists saying I couldn't do what I'd just done. They said the plants would fail. Well, the proof of the pudding is in the eating and, despite an abysmal month of weather, the plants not only survived but positively thrived. I was cutting fresh basil for weeks, and when Toby Buckland came down he was amazed at the sight of my supermarket seedlings doing so well. I can say, hand on heart, it is worth having a go, and that success is guaranteed if you split the plant and then protect it with a cloche. Or you can go the whole hog and not protect it. If you don't try it yourself you'll never know.

Basil likes lots of sunshine, ideally with protection from the harshest of the weather, and well-drained soil that doesn't dry out too quickly. If you fancy growing some from seed (only to top up your pre-grown supermarket seedlings, of course), sow in April onto the surface of your favourite potting compost and cover with either a thin layer of the same compost or a sprinkling of vermiculite. Once the seedlings are through and large enough to handle you can prick them out into individual 9 cm pots and grow them on until the weather warms up or there is a space in the greenhouse. They do grow well near tomatoes. I still prefer the idea of liberating supermarket seedlings, though.

PLANTING SUPERMARKET BASIL
1 Soak the supermarket bought pot basil for an hour or so before splitting. **2** I used my hands rather than a knife to rip the plant apart as the fibrous roots split easily. **3** I spaced each plant about 30 cm apart and put them straight in the ground. **4** Firm in the soil around the roots so the plant sits up nicely and water in well. Voila!

Greek basil has small leaves and seems to be tolerant of quite a lot of mistreatment. Actually, it isn't mistreatment but more like no treatment. It was one of the supermarket pots of living herbs I divided on camera. One pot contained lots of seedlings, so I simply knocked it out of the pot, divided it roughly into four and replanted. The plants were great in my raised beds. Once released from their confines, the plants grew to 20 cm (8 inches) high and looked like small, topiarized trees. I can imagine them growing really well in old containers.

If you can't get hold of plants from your supermarket, you can grow them from seed. Remember that basil will curl up and die at the merest mention of frost, so any sowings made in April will need to stay indoors on a sunny windowsill or in a heated greenhouse until May or June. You can sow directly outdoors in June and again in August. This last sowing will just about make decent plants before you either lift them or offer them up as sacrifices to Jack Frost. Just trim the plants to keep them looking tidy and use the trimmings in the kitchen.

CHERVIL
Cath loves fresh chervil and says it's difficult to buy. I sowed some alongside the coriander at the same time and it came up a treat.

CHIVES
I bought a pot of ready-grown chives, split them up and planted them directly into the soil about 25 cm (10 inches) apart. They can be used as a garnish or to add a hint of onion to dishes, and if left to flower have lovely mauve allium flowers.

CORIANDER
You need to keep a careful watch over coriander as it will quickly run to seed. The sure sign that it is on the way to flowering is when the new leaves start to look thin and feathery. And it does it so easily – if you move plants they run to seed, or if there is a cold spell, they run to seed. The best way to tackle this problem is to sow little and often and where you want it to grow. This means waiting until early summer to sow, and sowing into well-drained soil in a sunny spot. The good thing is that once you have a happy plant you can pick a lot of leaves. Picking also delays the onset of flowering. However, all is not lost if your plants do run to seed; wait until the flower heads stop smelling and the seed is ripe, then use some in the kitchen and save some for next year's crop.

DILL

I like these aniseed-flavoured plants and seeds, but I've got to say the plants can be temperamental to grow. It's best sown where you want it to grow, as the plant doesn't like being uprooted. Well-drained soil is best, so my raised beds did the job. If you sow a block or half a row every two weeks you will get a continuous supply of fresh leaves right through to autumn.

You can also wait for plants to flower if you like to use the seeds in your cooking. Cut off the flower heads and carefully place them in a paper bag. Put the bags, tied at the open end, in a warm place, such as an airing cupboard. After about a week the seeds will have fallen out and you can store them in any airtight container.

ROSEMARY

I got my first rosemary cuttings from Trevor, a plot holder who had got his from Manuel, owner of a beautifully tended plot on the site. They are now planted in a row with the aim of producing a low hedge of this wonderful herb. Gardeners can make a meal out of growing certain plants, and the propagation of rosemary is a case in point. Lots of textbooks and websites go into minute detail on how to raise plants from cuttings, almost wrapping it up in a green-fingered cloak of mystery. My plants? Manuel had snipped a few shoots, mostly 15 cm (6 inches) long, off his plants, given them to

1 Greek basil splits well from a supermarket pot too. **2** Chervil is easy to grow from seed, but hard to find fresh in shops. **3** Rosemary has a fabulous aroma and is an extremely versatile culinary herb.

Trevor who in turn potted them up; they rooted well and he gave them to me. I watered them in thoroughly because it was a dry day, and that was that. They took beautifully and are growing away happily. Maybe I got lucky, or maybe my clay soil was perfect for them, and I suppose the soil was warm, but whatever the reason for their success, I don't think there is an easier plant to acquire, grow and harvest from than Manuel's original rosemary. I hope it will last for decades to come. It should.

SAGE

Fresh sage is so much milder and, in my opinion, better tasting than the dried stuff you can buy, which tends to be bitter and has too concentrated a flavour. The purple, grey-green leaves are lovely to look at and are highly productive. Growing sage was a cinch. That's partly because it is so tolerant of lots of soil types, and all it needs is a good dose of sun every day. The soil

1 Sage is an evergreen herb and looks great spilling over the edge of my raised beds.
2 Alys gave Connie some pineapple sage. You only need to add a little to give a zing to salads.

in my raised bed was well drained and packed with nutrients, and the sage loved it. I planted small plants about 15 cm (6 inches) apart and soon they knitted together to form a thicket. In dry weather don't bother watering it as plants prefer tougher growing conditions.

You can also grow it from seed. Sow seeds indoors in March or outdoors in April and be prepared for a wait. Seed-raised plants won't be large enough to start picking from until the following July. When your plants have finished flowering, cut them back by half. This reduces the chance of damaged stems due to wind rock and can supply you with enough cuttings to furnish every plot on your site with this gorgeous plant. I grow the purple-leafed sage because it looks great and is perfect in the kitchen.

SWEET MARJORAM

If you can be bothered to grow this, it is a perennial. It's a bit demanding grown that way, though, as you have to bring plants indoors or into a warm greenhouse over winter. I think growing it fresh every year is best anyway, but there speaks a man without a greenhouse. Sow seeds indoors a month before your last frosts – May time should cover most areas. Prick out, harden off and plant into well-drained soil in a sunny position. In a warm summer plants will romp away and you will be picking sprigs of sweet marjoram whenever you need them. Always leave enough shoots on the plants to sustain growth, though. You can use the leaves fresh from the plant or dry them for use later.

THYME

I'll avoid the obvious jokes about never having enough thyme on the plot, and say that if you grow it hard, as Monty always told us, you wouldn't go far wrong. Don't over-water it, don't feed it and your thyme will be fine. You can grow from seed but plants can take a year or so to reach a reasonable size. The best way is to find a plot holder with an established clump and in early summer offer to divide the plant. This will result in two things: the first is a rejuvenated plant for the owner, the second lots of smaller plants for you and your neighbours. Lift the established plant and tear small chunks off, making sure each new plant has a portion of root and a few shoots. Get these planted as soon as possible into well-drained soil. The soil should not be too rich or plants will be leggy. Water them in, shade from excessive sun, and within a month you will see new shoots. There are lots of different 'flavours' of thyme, but I grow lemon-scented and the original variety. Both are excellent producers of fine foliage.

ROSETTE FENNEL

No, it isn't a new variety of fennel, but a good way to introduce one of the proudest moments on the plot.

During potato day we also ran a little produce competition, so I entered a few things in the different classes just for a bit of fun and to enter into the general spirit of the (extremely) amateur competition. I have never thought about growing to show as most veg shows are all about who can grow the biggest, longest or heaviest produce, which doesn't really interest me. It's also extremely difficult to do if you grow organically, as most growers use secret ingredients which are mainly made up of mad concoctions of various chemicals, making their produce inedible. But I genuinely thought my ninja fennel was a worthy entry into the open category of best in show.

Originally sown in my plastic growhouse at home in April, I planted out the small seedlings in early summer. Fennel doesn't like root disturbance, so be ultra-careful not to cause any damage when planting out. It is a crop from the Med and any cold weather can result in plants bolting. (This is when they produce flower heads instead of putting their efforts into the crop. If they do this, all is not lost, you can collect the seeds and use them in cooking or for the next sowing.) You could play safe and sow directly in the soil where the plants are to be harvested; this eliminates root disturbance, but keep a cloche handy if cold weather is forecast.

However you grow them, you can expect to be harvesting 15 weeks after sowing. Mine grew away nicely at the ends of each of the brassica rows. A plot holder had told me they could attract wasps, especially if they run to seed, so I guess he didn't have much faith in my gardening knowledge that wasps parasitize on caterpillars. The crop was one thing, but a reduction in the numbers of caterpillars on my caulis was a bonus. Ken loves to take the mickey out of me for being a yuppie and the fennel is what he describes as yuppie food, along with anything you wouldn't see on a standard plate of meat and two veg.

The fennel grew really well and on show day I carefully lifted one, washed the roots, and plonked it on the show table. I had two big surprises that day. The first was seeing the red rosette with first prize being awarded to me for the fennel, the second was seeing Brenda, my mother-in-law, entering pink fir apple potatoes from her allotment at our show!

⋯⟩
Just look at that fennel! What a beauty. I washed the roots off and placed it on the judging table. It quickly wilted in the heat, but just managed to hold on until the judges came round.

Joe's Veg Heroes
Carol Klein

Carol is a fantastic plantswoman and runs her own nursery in Devon. She is a co-presenter on *Gardeners' World* and also presented the extremely popular and inspiring *Grow Your Own Veg* on BBC2. She also writes regularly for many publications. Her enthusiasm for propagating and growing pretty much everything including edibles is infectious, and she always asks me how I'm getting on down the allotment.

Carol Klein

Veg garden Devon. The vegetable area of the garden is all raised beds covering approximately 200 square metres.

Soil type Heavy clay. It's extremely fertile but hard work.

Biggest growing problem Slugs. This year however I'm going to try a new deterrent – red bush leaves as a mulch, (also called Rooibos, these are a by-product of the South African tea industry), which I've heard do the job.

Time spent on vegetable growing Anything from half an hour to several hours a week depending on the time of year and how busy I am doing other things!

Favourite tool My mum's ladies border fork. Although I don't dig my raised beds I use it for loosing the soil before planting.

Favourite crop I love all the leaves. Swiss chard is my all-time favourite as it just goes on and on. You can crop it for most of the year and it's an efficient use of space. It always tastes so fresh and it looks great too.

Favourite time of year I love both spring and late summer. Spring is all about anticipation and seeing new shots emerging. Late summer is about harvesting and being rewarded.

What's your first memory of vegetable growing? Helping my grandad on his allotment. Although he mainly grew chrysanthemums, I helped him dig up some potatoes. I also helped my mum, who grew tomatoes in boxes in the back yard.

When did you first grow vegetables? Although I grew a few tomatoes and beans in pots on the balcony when I lived in Ladbroke Grove, I really started to grow my own in earnest when I moved to Devon in 1978. We moved so we could have a large garden and to grow food. I was inspired by a book called *Self Sufficiency* by John Seymour.

Why do you love growing fruit and vegetables so much? It's incredibly direct. It puts you in touch with something that's been going on for ever. It's something that humans have always done. Oh, and I just love food!

Why do you think growing your own is so important? Because you know precisely what you're eating. I grow what I want and know that there are absolutely no chemicals involved, which is of paramount importance to me as an organic gardener. I also love to eat everything as fresh as it can possibly be.

What do you do with your excess produce? Give it away. If I have plenty left over when I open my garden for the Yellow Book (National Garden Scheme) I sometimes sell it and the proceeds go to their charities.

What is the best piece of growing advice you've been given? Be patient. Charles Napier, my next door neighbour, was a vicar and a very keen vegetable grower. He gave me plenty of good advice during my early veg growing days.

What's the best advice you can give to other growers? I have two! Get to know and look after your soil; always see it as living stuff. Also, I always grow in modules, which means I can stagger planting and ensure a good succession of harvests.

Sowing outdoors

Early summer instinctively feels the right time for sowing and planting.
The soil is moist, the days are long, and the temperatures are usually good
enough to get most plants up and running. The temptation is to have
a mass sowing day where everything is sown, the whole plot covered and
at the end of the day you stand back and admire your handiwork. However,
when all the plants mature at the same time you will regret not sowing,
and planting, successionally. Although, however hard you try, you will
always get gluts of courgettes and beans, so I wouldn't worry too much
about staggering those.

Many crops can be sown directly into the soil early on in summer, just
make sure that you have removed as many weeds as possible from the
soil before sowing (although you won't get them all out) and that you have
hoed and raked the soil into a manageable state. Seeds won't grow through
lumps of clay or stone so remove these, too.

The day before you intend to sow it's a good idea to thoroughly water
the soil. This ensures that moisture is present around all the seeds, and
this will aid fast germination. If you can't get to your plot to water the
day before, you can water the planting holes or drills on the day of sowing,
but do let the water drain away before you actually drop in the seeds.

Once I have sown seed, I like to cover the drill or hole with compost.
This produces a great medium for the seeds to grow up through, which is
especially important if your soil is clay and forms a hard cap after watering.
It also marks the row, as invariably the compost is a different colour to
the soil. This will also help you to distinguish between weeds and your
seedlings later on. Some gardeners (those with a lot of windowsill space),
often sow a few seeds into a small plot for comparison purposes, but on
my plot the main weed is horsetail – and I can tell that a mile off.

Invariably seeds sown directly outside will produce root systems that
are stronger than those on plants grown in trays. Direct sown seeds are
free range from day one, and this has the benefit of reducing the amount
of watering needed later on in the year.

SQUASHES AND THINGS

Get your courgettes and cucumbers in the soil from early summer. Don't
sow too many as each plant will overload you with produce. Pumpkins can
also be sown now, or plants can be planted out. You can also put sweetcorn
seed directly into the soil as the warmer temperatures will mean the seeds

Pick courgettes whilst they're
young. They're so prolific
they'll just keep coming and
coming. If you leave them on
the plant for a week when
they're this size you'll be
coming back to a marrow!

germinate before they have a chance to rot. Runner and French beans can be sown, too, but you have to be wary of birds and slugs, as both love the tasty shoots as they emerge from the soil.

SALAD CROPS

All the salad-leafed crops can go in during early summer, but if you are sowing directly into the soil, do it in the late afternoon. Lettuce, for example, is very sensitive to high temperatures and will not grow if the soil is hot. Even waiting a few hours and sowing at 5pm will provide a cool spell in the evening and night to encourage successful germination. And that's an indication of how fast seeds can get going at this time of year.

The interest in salad leaves is going from strength to strength. We've all read reports on how many miles supermarket salads have travelled before reaching the shelves, and how concentrated the chlorine wash is to clean them of everything that might offend, so seed sales of these are growing exponentially.

Now I like salads, and fresh leaves are far superior in taste and longevity compared to shop-bought stuff. Picked from the plot, a bunch of leaves will keep for ten days and can then be easily rejuvenated by a quick wash in cold water. Supermarket bagged leaves often go off in three or four days. When harvesting lettuce and other leaves, just cut off what you need. The cut-and-come-again varieties will definitely produce more leaves – it's what they do best – whereas the stumps you leave behind when cutting headed lettuce often sprout tasty nibble-sized shoots.

I tried and grew a few good, hard-working varieties. Lollo Rossa, which has become a traditional variety that is hardy, doesn't seem to run to seed and has a great peppery taste. Younger leaves are milder than older, tougher leaves, though, so cut a few as you need them rather than a whole head at once. I also grew a few half rows of Little Gem to ensure a good continuous supply of lettuce heads. It tastes great and takes no time at all to form harvestable plants. If I didn't have an allotment I'd get a few in pots and containers at home. I always feel it is a bit of a cheat growing mixes of seeds, but I have to say that when it comes to lettuce, they are a great idea. You get the whole range of taste, colours and shapes from one packet and if you sow thickly you can eat the thinnings as you work the row.

ANNUAL ROCKET

Now this is technically a salad with its spicy nutty flavour, which I love eating with Parmesan cheese and a little olive oil – as long as it's spicy enough! It's

PLANTING YOUNG SALAD LEAVES
1 Salad leaves can be direct sown or sown into modules or small pots and grown on. **2** When the compost around the plant is wet, split into individual plants. **3** Plant around 25–30 cm apart and firm in well. **4** Always water newly planted plants, even if the soil is wet, to ensure good contact between the roots and soil.

one of those cut-and-come-again plants and the leaves taste best when small so it feels as if actually you're doing it a favour by cutting it back. It will germinate in quite cold weather but tends to bolt and run to seed if it gets too hot. Just keep sowing, that's what I say!

PAK CHOI

It used to be new and trendy, but now everyone seems to be growing pak choi, and for a couple of reasons. Firstly, because it is so tasty, and secondly, because it is easy to grow.

You can grow pak choi in two ways. One option is to broadcast-sow the seeds and harvest the leaves when they are around 6 cm (2.4 inches) high. This is classed as a cut-and-come-again method; you cut some and it comes up again a few weeks down the track. The second way to grow pak choi, and the way I did it, is to grow the plants to maturity, or until they have formed a head. This isn't a long-distance crop, as it only takes about eight weeks from sowing to harvesting. I broadcast sowed the seed directly onto the soil in mid-summer, spacing the seeds approximately 15 cm (6 inches) apart in each direction. They germinated within a week and the plants romped away. The root systems are shallow so the best way of watering, should you need to, is little and often. Drenching the plants will only waste water, as it will soon run out of the roots' reach.

The crop keeps its crunch better than your normal lettuce varieties, and the green-stemmed varieties are tastier than the white-stemmed ones. Another attribute of pak choi is its hardiness: you can sow all the way through summer, right into early autumn, cloche plants over and still have a crop throughout winter. In fact, it is better to wait until the longest day has passed and then sow, as there is less risk of plants bolting.

The only downside to pak choi is that it is open to all the usual brassica problems. However, unlike most brassicas, it is up and out of the ground before your average caterpillar has time to spot it. I didn't have any problems with my crop. I found that they also store for a long time at the bottom of the fridge and are so easy to cook. I just stir fried them for a couple of minutes in the wok with some garlic, soy sauce and sesame oil. Delicous.

My pak choi was a real success and we ate all that I produced. It's one of those plants that you can harvest over a pretty long period as you can eat the young plants to help thin them out, and the more mature ones last well in the ground too.

Summer maintenance

In the summer, maintenance is all about regularity, so little and often rather than the occasional blitz.

Now for most people, summer visits to the plot are a relaxing and laid back combination of weeding, sowing and harvesting – what I class as pottering jobs, which can be interspersed with chats to fellow plot holders and a sit down every now and then. For myself however, it's a time when things really pick up as I film the RHS shows and I tend to zoom round the country filming whatever's looking good in the gardening world.

Cathy and the kids helped out a lot when I was away working, and it was a wet summer which certainly reduced watering, but did increase weeding. The most important thing in the summer months is to try and stay focussed and pragmatic whilst you're on your plot, which in my case meant having to keep my head down and make the most of my time, even if it did mean being a little antisocial at times – apologies to all.

Watering

Even in the wettest of summers there are days when you need to water. I was glad I had sorted the water butts at the back of the shed because it gave me a natural source of water as opposed to the dip tank at the front of the plot. I do like the dip tank, as it is convenient for most of the year, but the natural rainwater collected from the shed roof seems better for the plants. I might be wrong.

Watering isn't difficult. If you want to make sure your plants and seeds get off to a good start, water them in well to get them established and they should do all the work for you. It's only when you encourage surface rooting by watering little and often that you create a rod for your own back (except with pak choi, where the roots are shallow and need watering little and often).

It's always best to water as early as you can in the morning, preferably as the sun comes up. This allows as much water as possible into the roots before any is lost to evaporation and the plants are put under stress. The next best time is watering in late evening. The same theory applies – lots of roots getting lots of water – but you do run the risk of encouraging some fungal diseases to multiply in the damp, cooler conditions. I reckon slugs would like it too. Most gardeners say you shouldn't water during the day, especially around midday, because the sun is high and strong and will evaporate water from the soil surface, and any splashes on leaves will act as magnifying glasses, burning holes into them. But I still say that watering a dying plant at high noon is better than not watering at all.

The key to reducing the need to water so often is getting your soil in good shape for the growing season. We are lucky on our site because we can get our hands on tonnes of council compost. I'm not kidding when I say that without that compost my plot would have produced next to nothing. Either that or it would have cost a fortune.

Failing that, the two best things you can do is to hoe and mulch. Hoeing not only slices off weeds that then dry and bake in the sun on the soil's surface, but it also produces a dust capping that will conserve moisture in the soil. In addition, it breaks up the capillary action of water, preventing it from moving towards the surface of the soil and evaporating.

Watering may not be an art but it is beginning to sound like a science. Remember, mulching with anything organic helps retain water in the soil, but only if the soil is moist to start with.

1 Watering thoroughly and deeply is important as a light spray will only draw roots up to the surface and weaken the plant. **2** I'm lucky to have a dip tank next to my plot, which I use during the driest spells when my own stored water has run out.

Holiday cover

Someone was supposed to look after my allotment whilst I was away, but didn't! I do know that Ken and Keith helped out a bit, though (thanks, chaps). If you can get someone in to look after your plot just for an hour or two every week, do! Here are some other tips you may find handy if you're planning a trip away.

- Plan your sowing to avoid crops maturing in your holidays.
- Give it a good weeding before you go.
- Pick any crops before you go – even if crops are slightly immature.
- Water well.
- Mulch when the soil is moist.
- Check every plant for signs of pest attack and do something about it before you go away.
- Pick off all diseased or peaky-looking leaves to prevent fungal problems.
- Ensure all structures. e.g. canes and wigwams, are secure to prevent wind damage.
- Earth up potatoes and ease soil around carrots to prevent greening of crops as they develop.
- If you have to plant out seedlings, make sure you water them well. They should last until you get back.
- Net everything that might be attacked, because it will be. If you don't net it, you don't get it.

Many people have greenhouses on their allotments, and this can cause an additional worry for growers going on summer holidays. While chatting to a plot holder on another site who was due to go on holiday, he told me what he did to ensure his greenhouse was okay while he was away.

By its very nature, all plants in the greenhouse are dependent on you for water, so he reduced their requirement by putting up shading – paint on and rub off shading is quickest and cheapest to use. Then he moved his plants to the shadier side of the greenhouse and put a large bucket of water near the plants so that the water would evaporate, increasing the humidity of the air around the plants, which in turn reduces the amount of water lost by them. He also puts old sacking on the greenhouse floor and thoroughly soaks it the day he goes on holiday. This is a version of the technique known as 'damping down', which again helps to increase the humidity of the air in the greenhouse, reducing the plants' stress on hot days.

--->
Keith was a builder and just loves designing gadgets and recycling anything he can. He made loads of these to water his tomatoes evenly and to draw their roots down deep into the soil.

Drip water feeders are also available for watering pot-grown plants in the greenhouse, and containers outside, but they cost a fair few quid. Nothing, he says, beats the help of a friendly and green-fingered fellow plot holder.

Or you could do as Peter Whiting does: never go on holiday in the main growing season.

PRETTY STUFF

I know that many allotments are purely food factories, but I wanted to make mine look good too. Ken, a fellow plot holder, helped this cause when he challenged my children and all the other kids on the plot to a sunflower-growing competition. It was simple: the tallest sunflower won.

Ken supplied everyone who wanted to take part with a plant raised from the same batch of seed. Then it was everyone for themselves. Sunflowers want to grow tall, but there are ways to persuade them to grow even taller. They need to be started early by sowing seeds indoors and they will not stand up to frosts, so planting out has to wait until late spring, but preferably early summer. You can direct-sow seeds, but if the ground is cold and wet they can rot. Once up they need support, even at an early stage. The leaves are large and any wind can cause the stems to snap.

So it was one plant for Stan and one for Connie. We duly dug planting holes and loaded them with Ken's special compost mix (yeah, right, Ken, straight out of the bag!). Both sprinkled fish, blood and bone into the planting hole and mixed it in well. Mini triangles were placed on top and more compost was added. The plants then went into this mix. Unfortunately Stan snapped his plant on day one, but Ken kindly supplied a replacement.

The plants grew well and whenever we went up to the plot the plants were well watered. Stouter supports were added and soon both plants were towering hulks. Connie's plant was much taller than Stan's, but Ken's grandson's was even taller. Now,

I'm not making excuses, because I don't know how other people grew theirs, but ours were organic and never fed with anything stronger than fish, blood and bone. They were at the front of the plot where there is no shade so got every ray of sun in the dismal summer. Three metres was okay, but it wasn't tall enough. I must remember to pay Ken the wager next time I see him …

So, just in case you get roped into a competition, here are Swifty's top tips for nearly-prizewinning sunflowers:

- Start off with a tall-growing variety – Russian Giant is a good one.
- Sow indoors and plant out in early summer.
- Plant into a sunny position only.
- Put plenty of organic matter into the soil before planting.
- Never allow the plants to dry out.
- Stake them from day one and don't over tighten the twine (Stan!).
- Add a bit of fertilizer if you are really keen – fish, blood and bone is a good all-round fertilizer, or get it going with dried blood later on.
- Never bet too much on the outcome, as who knows what can happen on an allotment!

Then there were dahlias. There was nothing competitive about these gorgeous plants, just bucketloads of tradition. I always imagined including dahlias in my allotment at the planning stage and suddenly I was planting some out.

Once again, they are a crop that will not stand any amount of frost, so wait until early

----

1 OK, so you can dry the seeds and eat them, but let's face it, sunflowers are all about brightening up the allotment and growing the biggest one you can. They were my favourite flowers when I was a kid and now they are all over again. 2 The dahlias and rudbeckias near the shed really cheered us up in the summer and next year we'll certainly grow more flowers. Who knows, we may even grow some that aren't yellow!

summer before planting out. I actually picked up my tubers from a DIY store right at the end of spring. Although they were smallish tubers, they were worth a try. I lined an old fish crate with a thick wad of newspaper and then filled the crate with multipurpose compost. I nuzzled the tubers into it and added more compost to just about cover them. I watered the crate and placed it in the hallway of my house. Light isn't important at this stage, but a constantly warm temperature is essential. The idea was to get a few roots out of the tubers and even a couple of shoots before planting them out into the plot. Once the

first early potatoes were lifted, the dahlias would go in to replace them – right in front of the shed. Shed, dahlias, potatoes – the plot was feeling like a real allotment.

I added a few spadefuls of compost to improve the soil. The tubers, with roots but not so many shoots, were then carefully planted. After two weeks shoots had appeared, and by the end of summer there were buckets of dahlias to add to my burgeoning harvest. Next year I might try some from seed. I plan to start the seed off indoors and again plant out when all the frosts have finished.

Seasonal problems

As well as summer being the time when the allotment really came together, it was also the time when some things started to go wrong. Up until then I had been looking at the bigger picture of getting the plot up and running, but the season taught me just how important it is to look closer too.

For a start the areas I had covered with blue tarpaulin in the hope of keeping weeds at bay, were now causing problems of another kind. The tarpaulin had created the perfect breeding ground for slugs, which loved the heat and moisture it was retaining. To my horror, I found loads of the slippery creatures under there, happily living and breeding together and forming a small army of green eating machines. Needless to say, I immediately lifted up the tarpaulin, put it aside and squashed all the slugs I could see. *Hasta la vista*, slimeballs!

On another day Dr Ian Bedford, a professional entomologist (or 'bugman', as I called him), came up to look around my plot for pests and diseases. By the time he left I was pretty depressed at what he had found, but I'd learned so much from him that I'll be far more on the ball next year. I discovered that some of my brassica leaves were being eaten by cabbage white caterpillars. I had netted the plants to stop the pigeons eating them, but it wasn't fine enough to keep the butterflies out. I should have taken it off sooner to allow small birds, blue tits in particular, to feed on the caterpillars.

Ian also showed me an aphid-transmitted virus on some of my peas. Fortunately they were still cropping well and fine to eat, but some of the plants were going yellow. If I had caught the greenfly earlier I would probably have got away with this and had healthier, longer producing plants from which I could have saved and dried some peas to plant next season. As it was, I'd certainly be buying some new packets next year.

One thing that hits you in the summer months is what I call 'allotment envy'. You wonder how everyone else's plots can look so beautiful, healthy and weed free, whilst yours is still a bit of a mess. Manuel's allotment is always an absolute picture, and in my opinion the most beautiful plot on our site. He had thyme edging around his beds, huge quantities of marrows, pumpkins and squashes, and lush arches of beans and peas. I tried to quash my inadequate feelings by reminding myself that it was only my first year, and the others have a lot more time to spend on their plots than I do. But although it can feel like a knock back, I do like taking a look at the other plots. It can be educational and inspiring, and as a result I for one already have many ideas as to how to make mine look better next year.

SOME WAYS OF DEALING WITH DREADED SLUGS AND SNAILS ORGANICALLY

- Hand pick from plants, ideally at dusk on damp days.
- They don't like to cross copper, so use strips on the edges of raised beds.
- Scatter coffee grounds or sharp grit around young seedlings.
- Beer traps – cut plastic bottles in half, set the bottom part into the ground and fill, with the lip slightly above ground level (to stop beetles wandering in) with stale beer. Empty every morning!
- Use a parasitic nematode solution. Widely available in a dehydrated form, but the soil needs to be a minimum of 5ºC (41ºF) for them to work.
- Trap them under the domes of emptied-out half grapefruit skins.
- Place fresh comfrey leaves next to seedlings as they don't like to cross the coarse leaves.
- Let Keith's chickens loose on your plot every now and then as they are good slug eaters!

Rusty garlic

A fellow plot holder, who shall remain nameless, told me that the rust on my garlic was caused by a fungus called Puccini! It's actually a fungus called *Puccinia allii* and it causes rusty leaves on garlic, chives, onions and shallots. It took hold over my plants in the space of a couple of days in June, and seeing Manuel's and Keith's garlic succumb was no consolation.

The spores can be passed from plant to plant very easily. Wind and rain disperse spores, and even touching an infected plant and then touching your own plants will do the same. Spores can even be carried on harvested bulbs, so replanting from your own stock can compound the problem.

The good news is that even though it looks awful, if the plants have got going and already produced a bulb, chances are they will continue to grow and produce a decent crop. Infected leaves should not be composted, as the spores will survive the heat from an average heap. Burn them instead, if you are allowed.

Avoid infection in the first place by making sure there's plenty of potash in the soil. One plot holder on my site uses wood ash, while many have suggested burying comfrey leaves in the soil before planting. I might try both in future. The Royal Horticultural Society told me not to over-manure or add anything high in nitrogen to the soil where alliums (garlic, chives, onions and shallots) are going to be grown. Looking at last year's photographs, I might have planted the garlic too close together and then allowed other plants to restrict air and sun getting to the plants. Plenty of fresh air around the leaves is best for strong growth. I am going to space them out a bit more in the future – it's not as if the plot is a small one.

The last tip I was given was to buy fresh cloves every year and plant them in a different position just in case some spores overwinter in the soil.

Cabbages and caterpillars

It seems the whole brassica family are hard work. Once you've prepared the soil and planted the plants, a whole army of pests and diseases come along and try to thwart your efforts.

Caterpillars are the number one enemy, and damage to your brassicas can most likely be laid at the door of the cabbage white butterfy. From mid-summer onwards they flit around the plot looking for their victims. Actually, they look for and sniff out your plants. The butterflies are easy to spot, but their eggs are usually hidden on the undersides of brassica leaves, where within days they hatch out into caterpillars. They stay in their clusters and demolish a fully-grown leaf overnight.

1 Whitefly is easy enough to spot as long as you look on the underside of leaves. They can weaken plants but can easily be wiped off by hand. **2** This is what I came back to after my holidays! Tomato blight is pretty devastating and almost impossible to control.

When you grow brassicas you will come across one or all of the three main types of caterpillar:

🍃 Small white butterfly: look for single, orange-coloured eggs on the undersides of leaves. Eggs hatch into yellowish caterpillars with black markings along their backs.

🍃 Cabbage white butterfly: look for clutches of orange-coloured eggs on the undersides of leaves. Similar caterpillars to the small white will emerge.

🍃 Cabbage moth: more clutches of eggs on the undersides of leaves that hatch into small, chubby, green caterpillars.

Have no illusions about it, brassicas equal trouble. I should know, as caterpillars devoured many plants on my plot this year. Most plot holders recommend constructing a cage of fine mesh netting to keep the butterflies out. It makes sense, but it costs money and it can be fiddly taking the cages off every time you want to weed or water. A walk-in cage of butterfly-proof netting is the utopia of allotmenteers, but that's an expensive option.

The best and cheapest alternative is weekly vigilance. I got into the habit of spending a quarter of an hour every Sunday evening on egg-squashing duty. It's horrid, but when you think about how clean your eventual crop will be it makes up for orange-stained fingers.

Another method I keep hearing about is to use a rhubarb spray to deter butterflies. When you pick your rhubarb, strip the leaves from the stalks and soak the leaves in a dustbin full of water. Keep the brew covered and give it an occasional stir. Keep doing this until the stench from the brew makes your eyes water, then use a watering can to pour the neat liquid over the leaves of your brassicas. You'll need to repeat the watering after heavy rain.

Many plot holders also mix and match their crops to disguise their vulnerable plants (see Companion planting, page 76). Try planting marigolds in between your brassicas to stop butterflies and moths from spotting your crops. It has to be worth a try.

Bad old blighty

Potato and tomato blight is the same thing. It affects all solanum species, including ornamental plants, and it isn't a disease you can make light of. Having been responsible for the potato famine in the late 1840s, potato blight is still around and can cause havoc on your plot. It's all down to a fungus called *Phytophthora infestans* that strikes in humid, warm air conditions. When the air temperature doesn't get below 10°C (50°F) and feels sticky there is a high chance the fungus will strike.

TOMATO BLIGHT

Tomato blight was absolutely awful last year, and affected most tomatoes grown outside up and down the country. Indoor-grown tomatoes tend to be safer as the disease is spread by wind and rain splashing.

I only had a few plants that were struck down alarmingly quickly, but on my site many people's crops got the dreaded blight. Keith had got into tomatoes in such a big way I thought he was supplying Heinz for their ketchup! He lost pretty much all of them and was pretty distraught. I could tell at that moment he felt like giving up. I think it was his new-found love for his four chickens that saw him through those difficult times.

Tomato blight can affect the foliage, stems and fruit of tomatoes and the warning signs are dark spots with concentric rings which develop on older leaves first, but which quickly spread to the whole plant and affect the fruit. There aren't any known completely resistant varieties, although some of the cherry tomatoes are more resilient.

POTATO BLIGHT

With spuds, you'll know if you have blight because the tips of the leaves will start to turn brown and then black. The leaflets that make up the leaves then curl up and die. Brown patches will probably appear on the stems of the potatoes, and within a fortnight whole plants will collapse.

This is obviously critical to crop production, but when blight strikes late, as is so often the case in late summer conditions in the UK, the fungus can infect the tubers that have already formed. Then there's trouble. The skin of the potato is slightly darkened and there is a reddish-brown rot through the flesh. The easiest test is the smell of the rot – it is evil; once sniffed, never forgotten. Your crop is finished.

There are ways and means of reducing the effects of potato blight, and growing varieties that are resistant to the disease was my main strategy. Sarpo varieties have an in-built resistance and on my allotment they were great. Sarpo Axona, Una and Mira all stood up brilliantly when blight was around and produced heavy, great-tasting crops. They are maincrop varieties (the ones most susceptible to blight), so another good tip is to only grow early varieties, as these are planted, harvested and out of the ground before conditions are right for blight. If you want to live a little more dangerously, fellow plot holders and the bods at the Royal Horticultural Society have told me that Cara, Kondor, Markies and Valor have some in-built resistance, while Arran Comet, Arran Pilot, Epicure, Foremost, Golden Wonder, Home Guard, Majestic, and Ulster Chieftain are particularly susceptible to potato blight.

There are other ways to reduce the severity of blight, and it all starts when you buy in your seed potatoes. Even with certified seed stock bought from garden centres or mail order, it is worth checking them over for signs of blight. Inspect each one before planting and if there are any you are not happy with, any with darkened patches on the skin, don't bother planting them. I was told not to save seed potatoes from previous years, or in my case accept seed potatoes from other plot holders who have saved a few to replant. They might contain blight and could even carry virus problems – altogether a different story. Later in the year, be aware of the conditions in which blight will thrive and watch out for signs of an outbreak.

If you do suspect blight is attacking, nip out infected leaflets or leaves to prevent the spread of spores to the rest of the plant, crop or neighbouring plots. Don't compost these leaves: it's best to seal them in a plastic bag and put them out with the household refuse. Do not put them in your green recycling bin.

Just to be safe, make sure you earth up your developing stems as this can prevent spores of the fungus reaching the tubers. Even if blight strikes, you can still get a decent crop of spuds.

At the end of the season, when you are harvesting all your potatoes, make sure you don't leave any in the soil (believe me, this is difficult), and absolutely never leave infected potatoes by the side of the path or raised beds as these can cause re-infection the following year.

Blight does occur to varying degrees every year, so my advice to any new plot holder is to be aware of it and act quickly if you spot it. Oh, and check how resistant to blight the variety of potato you want to grow is in the first instance – they are all different.

PLOT ESSENTIALS – SUMMER

If you have one day a week at the plot, make sure you:

- Water, if dry and in hot weather, and mulch with compost.
- Hoe.
- Sow short rows or small blocks of seeds.
- Check for pests.
- Harvest anything that is looking near maturity.
- Get in with your neighbours for holiday cover.

Joe's Veg Heroes
Monty Don

Monty was the main presenter on *Gardeners' World* between 2003 and 2008, and has presented several gardening programmes, including *Fork to Fork* – which was based on his own experiences of growing and cooking food. He has also written many gardening books extolling the virtues of growing organic fruit and vegetables. He is so passionate it becomes infectious. It was he who encouraged me to have a go with the container vegetable garden and he has always supported me and my allotment. Thanks, Monty!

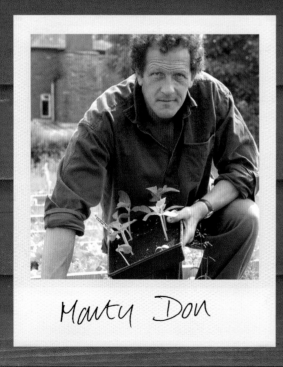

Monty Don

Veg garden, Herts The whole garden is 2 acres.

Soil type Clay loam.

Biggest growing problem Lack of time.

How much time do you spend on your plot? Not enough.

Favourite tool My stainless steel spade; because it is perfect in every spade-like way.

Favourite crop Cos lettuce.

Favourite time of year April, because everything seems possible.

What's your first memory of vegetable growing? Stealing strawberries from under the netting and getting stuck! It must have been around 1959, when I was four.

When did you first grow vegetables?
I helped in the garden from the age of about seven, and took over entire responsibility for the vegetables when I was 17. We were pretty much self-sufficient in veg, so it meant growing a wide range.

Why do you love growing fruit and vegetables so much? What is there not to love? I suppose it is an atavistic connection with the land and the completely honourable peasant mentality, that was lost in Britain with the Industrial Revolution, yet persists in our gardens and allotments. Growing food for your family and friends is a basic human instinct.

Why do you think growing your own is so important? For a start it connects you with food in a way that is closer and more immediate than anything else. It also provides a local, seasonal supply that is cheaper and more convenient than any other source. And usually better. And, of course, it is deeply, deeply enjoyable.

What do you do with your excess produce? Compost most of it. Some goes to the chickens and we freeze or otherwise preserve and store as much as we possibly can so there is very little conspicuous excess. If we go to friends' houses for dinner I always take a box of veg as a present.

What is the best piece of growing advice you've been given? 'Better to be late than early, because you can always catch up at the back end.' In other words, avoid the temptation to fill the veg garden with seeds and seedlings at the first sign of spring – which nearly always ends in disaster – because once the ground warms up things will grow fast, and anyway, the growing seasons lasts much longer into autumn than most people realize.

What's the best advice you can give to other growers? Grow what you like to eat and get the compost heap going.

Why do you think allotments are so important? They provide an opportunity for those without either a garden, or space within their garden, to grow vegetables and fruit and thereby connect with the seasons, create a supply of fresh, seasonal food, share the community of other growers and become part of the ancient need to feed ourselves. This latter point – feeding ourselves rather than passively accepting what others supply us – is becoming increasingly important and relevant, and as a result allotments will become increasingly vital as a food source, as well as providing pleasure and leisure. I've never had an allotment myself, but I've seen hundreds, especially from the train from Hampshire to Waterloo!

Autumn at the plot

When I got back from my summer holiday I was in for a real shock. Mark, my director and man behind the invisible voice, was supposed to keep an eye on my allotment while I was away on my rather generous, but much-needed three-week holiday. Well, to cut a long story short and avoid any unpublishable expletives, it turned out he hadn't been down there once and I came back to a sea, or should I say, an ocean, of weeds.

Fortunately, being a typical British summer it had apparently rained pretty much every day so the watering wasn't an issue. I suppose it taught me a lesson. You simply can't leave your plot with anyone else and expect them to treat it as you would. It's a lot of hard work and only you will be truly passionate about it and prepared to put in the hours and graft to make it work. If you look after it on a regular, ongoing basis, you can keep on top of it, but once it starts to get out of hand it is extremely difficult to get it back into shape. I spent a solid day and half up there, weeding and digging, just to get back on track.

Anyway, that aside, on my return from holiday the seasons began to change rapidly. Moving into autumn gave the plot a very different feel, but, more importantly, a different pace too. I knew that this would be the last time this year that I would have to weed out the visible horsetail, as it had finally slowed down so much it had almost stopped growing. What a huge relief – I could stop chasing my tail until the following spring.

Spring and summer had been hectic; I'd never once quite felt in total control and never knew precisely what was around the corner. In autumn the tempo is dictated by the shortening of the days, the dropping of the temperatures and, fortunately, making things generally far, far slower. It felt as if I'd been on a long distance run but was now walking home and getting my breath back.

Autumn is a fabulous season at the plot. There's still plenty of produce to harvest, but there is a marked change as leeks, squashes and even my rasberries started producing, whilst plants such as the calabrese just kept going on and on right through the season.

Season of change and fruitfulness

Once I got the plot ship-shape and looking good again I immediately felt in control. I looked back at the whole plot and realised just how far I'd come from day one. In fact, I went home that night and looked at some photos of the plot when it was covered in weeds before I took it on. It felt like a huge achievement and also reinforced why I loved gardening; you can visibly see the results of the hard work you put in and experience the very real transformation of a space.

Sure, I had designed many gardens over the years, and built many too, but this was somewhere I had worked and converted pretty much myself. I had created a productive allotment providing plenty of food for all the family, which was also an attractive place to want to go and enjoy at every available opportunity. I also reflected on how much I had learned over the year – I'd gone from a complete novice to someone who now knew how to grow a wide range of produce. I felt on top of the world.

After patting myself on the back (well someone's got to do it!), I decided to make the most of the autumn and get on with some of those jobs that needed doing.

As I cut down finished crops my compost heap finally started to stack up. Building my three-bay heap out of old pallets was one of the first jobs I did on the site, but of course it had very little in it, apart from one bay which was filled with some of the council compost. In fact, looking back it's one of those jobs that I could really have left until late autumn or even winter if needed, and just heaped the compostable material out of the way somewhere until I got round to building it.

Now the pallets were surrounded by horsetail and had bindweed growing up the outside of them. Of course it's important not to get any weed roots into the compost, so I cleaned it out as well as I could. I then cut back my comfrey hard to the ground and added those leaves to the compost. I then dug up all the comfrey plants and planted them in a line on the outside of the compost bins. This is a far more sensible spot for them to be anyway, as it's out the way and near the water butts, so I can easily make a liquid comfrey feed and chuck any leftover foliage straight into the compost.

I also dug a new bean pit for the following year, moving it away from where it had been. I'd been advised to do this on the basis that if you dig

···⟶

1 Sweet potatoes come in all shapes and sizes! **2** Carol Klein gave me some ruby Chard, which looks as good as it tastes. **3** The ever generous Manuel gave me some Jerusalem artichokes after mine failed. **4** Another couple of meals for the family sorted. Leek and potato soup anyone?

a pit in the late summer or early autumn you can directly chuck in some of the old waste foliage you are removing, and this will rot down over the winter, ready for spring planting.

The sunflower competition had rather fizzled out by now, only because most of the sunflowers were now being eaten by a flock of emerald green parakeets! They are a surreal sight in Enfield, I can assure you, but there are over 30,000 of them in and around London and, believe me, they don't half eat a lot! Ken and I officially closed the competition giving first prize to 'the chap with the curly hair'. Connie came third and Ken's grandson, Ben, and Stanley brought up the rear.

My basil experiment had gone so well that I harvested all the plants before the first frost got them and made up a load of pesto sauce to keep us going. (If you cover it with a layer of olive oil in the jar it seals it in and it lasts even longer.)

One disappointment, however, was my sweet potatoes. I harvested mine the same day as the RHS did at Hyde Hall. The leaves had been slightly frosted with some colder weather forecasted, so it seemed the ideal time to lift them. The strange thing was that the RHS had a bumper crop but I only managed a trug full from all my plants. I can only put it down to the soil – I had dug it well and incorporated plenty of organic matter, but underneath lay a clay pan. I hadn't had time to double-dig, and so some of the tubers came up bent, which was a sign that they had hit something hard and double backed on themselves. They obviously need a deeper soil for a better crop. We had enough for our family but I was really hoping I'd have loads to give away to the other plot holders, as a way of thanking them for everything they had helped me out with over the year.

Breaking new ground

One part of the plot that I hadn't dealt with at all up until then was the whole width of the bottom end, near the main grass path. It was still covered in weeds and had pretty much merged into the main path between the allotments altogether. Before now I had only thrashed at them and hoed in anger every now and then just to keep them down, but I really wanted to tackle this precious space to make room for some Brussels sprouts. I wanted the Brussels to be ready for Christmas, but I knew when they were going in that I'd probably missed that boat. Oh well, January sprouts are just fine by me. In fact, any sprouts are fine by me as long as they're not over-boiled and soggy.

Digging over this area of soil, which hadn't been touched since rotavation day, helped me make the conscious decision that I would never use a rotavator on the plot again. No, I hadn't suddenly seen the error of my ways – looking back on how much I'd produced over the year I knew there's no way I would have come that far without the machine – but from now on, as most of the infrastructure was in, I could cope with it all by thorough hand digging.

This area is actually one of my best areas for soil, but I still used the special brassica mix when planting as it had worked a treat on all the others. A few weeks after planting I checked on all the plants. Some had a few holes developing in the leaves, and sure enough I found quite a few cabbage white caterpillars nestled in the heart of a few of the plants, so I immediately squished them. I was now looking far closer than before, just as many experienced vegetable growers had advised me, and hopefully by doing so I avoided a lot of damage.

I stood in my shed and looked out across the plot. I had come full circle. Last year I had to phone Monty for advice, but now I knew exactly what I was doing.

Autumn fruit

In my first year fruit was very much low in my list of priorities. I would recommend to anyone taking over a plot for the first time that this should be the case. The reason is that planting fruit is a long term project. A young maiden apple tree can take a few years to produce anything and you have to be sure you like the plot and have the time and energy to keep it on. After a year I knew that I needed more fruit.

First of all check with your council or whoever runs the site that you are actually allowed to plant fruit trees. Sure, raspberries and soft fruit will be fine, but apples, pears and cherries might be different. They are considered permanent planting and are frowned on by many councils. Don't ask me why. I suppose they take up space and could cast shadows on other plots, especially if left unpruned. It's simply safer to ask before you plant.

RASPBERRIES

Autumn was a significant time for *Gardeners' World* too, as we now had a new presenter in Toby Buckland, who had taken over the mantle from Monty. Toby has had an allotment for years and was keen to come down and see mine. I think he was planning on having a real laugh at my expense, but when he got there he actually seemed genuinely impressed with what I'd achieved.

Of course, whilst he was round I had to rope him into helping me build a frame for my raspberries, which was another fixture on the plot that overall made it look more permanent and better organized.

We constructed a double-fence system using strong fence posts and galvanized wire. Two 2 metre (6.6 foot) posts were driven into the ends of the rows, cross bars were screwed midway and also near to the top of each post, and wires run from end to end. The raspberry canes could then easily be tied in to the wire to prevent wind rock and damage. I had planted the autumn-fruiting 'Autumn Bliss', which is one of the highest-yielding autumn-fruiting varieties and it was still providing firm fruits of good flavour. These plants are sturdy and so hadn't needed support. I was also growing the summer-fruiting Glen Ample, which produces masses of deep red fruit that are tasty and can be frozen, although mine hadn't produced anything in their first year. However, I have high hopes for next year.

Toby also helpfully explained succinctly the difference in pruning these two types. Basically, he told me you should treat the autumn fruiters like herbaceous plants and cut them back to the ground each February, whereas with the summer fruiters you only cut back the canes that have borne fruit that year. Simple as that.

Autumn is actually a great time to plant as you can pick up raspberry canes as bare-rooted plants. (These are plants that have been grown in the field by nurseries and sold on unpotted and without soil on their roots.) They are usually cheaper than pot-grown specimens – and can be better plants.

Raspberries can be divided according to their fruiting times. You get either summer- or autumn-fruiting.

Use string rather than wire to tie in raspberry canes as it won't cut the stems. Wrap the string around the wire frame a couple of times first to stop them sliding around.

SUMMER-FRUITING RASPBERRIES

- Most popular
- Fruit in July and August
- Fruit is produced on last year's canes
- Strong wires and supports are essential
- Can be grown in most parts of the UK
- Prune canes down straight after fruiting
- Birds devour anything that isn't netted

AUTUMN-FRUITING RASPBERRIES

- Becoming well known
- Fruit in September until the first frosts
- Fruit is produced on the tips of this year's canes
- Support isn't essential, but is beneficial
- Best in milder areas of the UK
- Cut all canes down in February
- You can often get away with little or no bird damage

STEPOVERS

A good way to overcome any height restrictions on an allotment is to grow low-growing fruit. I'm thinking of stepover apples and pears. These are exactly what they sound like – low growing horizontal branches form low hurdles of fruit. They require some training and it will take two or three years to form anything like a barrier, but they do look good.

FAMILY TREES

Stepovers on an allotment may be a design element too far for many (Ken's still getting his head around diamond-shaped beds so I'd better leave stepovers alone for a year or two) but family trees should be acceptable. These are mainly apple trees where three or sometimes four different varieties of apple have been grafted onto one root stock. Obviously you get a choice of apple over a period of time, and all from one tree. You can buy them from most garden centres, but if you really want to splash out there are specialist fruit nurseries that will graft the varieties of your choice onto the root stock of your choice. How about that for the ultimate in bespoke apples? Obviously it will cost.

FRUIT PESTS

Whatever fruit you choose to grow, something will attack. I've quickly learnt this on the allotment. Your soft fruit will be prize targets for birds. Ideally you can create a fruit cage to protect the fruit. A few pieces of timber and strong netting will do the job. More expensive are off-the-shelf walk-in cages. The tubular plastic structure is easy to put up, but the bill is high. Draping netting onto your raspberries is not a good idea as the birds will simply sit on the net and peck away. There is also the danger of birds getting caught up in the net, so be aware. It's also good to let birds in and around developing plants as they can pick off bugs, but keep them out as the fruit starts to form.

Your top fruit – pears, apples and the like – are usually less liable to be attacked. Frost can damage early blossom so a large piece of fleece might come in handy in spring.

Fruit propagation

Most of the crops on the plot are grown from seed or from plants bought in and planted. But once you have some fruit you can make more of it for free.

STRAWBERRIES

Strawberries are fantastic at producing more plants for nothing. They send out long runners with small plants attached to the ends. When the small plants come into contact with the soil they naturally produce roots. This is clever as the parent plants send out runners a couple of feet away and therefore produce the next generation without creating competition for themselves. You can help this along by pegging down the small plants to ensure they come into good contact with the soil. A split cane, piece of wire or even a hair pin (I don't actually use many of them myself!) pushed over the runner will do the job. Better still is to sink a pot of compost beneath the small plant and peg the plant into the surface of the soil. Once roots have formed you can separate, or cut, the umbilical cord and your new plant is away on its own roots. It's a good way of keeping your stocks fresh as strawberries are prone to diseases. Renewing your plants every three years is good fruit-growing practice.

1 Strawberries are one of the easiest plants to propagate. Just pot up the runners or plant them straight into the ground. **2** Once you have raspberry plants you've got them for life. You can increase your stock by cutting off and replanting the suckers.

RASPBERRIES

Raspberries are a family favourite and it is easy to get new plants from your existing stock. In fact, your plants are probably trying to produce fresh plants right now. They form suckers which root along the length of the underground stems. All you need to do is lift one from the soil, trace the stem back 30 cm (12 iches) or so and sever with your secateurs. The plant, or cutting, you remove should have healthy leaves and a good length of stem along which there are plenty of roots. Replant into prepared soil and off you go – a new raspberry plant for free and a tidy up of your existing stock into the bargain. Only detach runners from plants that look healthy. This is best done in October and November.

BLACKBERRIES

Chances are you will have a spare plot on your site that is covered in blackberries. If you want some on your plot dig a 15 cm (6 inch) hole and bury the tip of a blackberry shoot in it. Refill the hole with soil, tread down and hold any springy shoots in place with a bent piece of wire. Do this in July. This tip will root and by the following July you will be able to cut off the rooted tip, and replant elsewhere on the plot.

BLACKCURRANTS

Home-grown blackcurrants are good and the plants are easy to propagate. Again, make sure you choose healthy plants and cut 25 cm (10 inch) cuttings from this season's wood. Do this in October. The cuttings need to be the thickness of a pencil. Make a sloping cut at the top of the cutting – this allows water to run off the cut end – and a straight cut just beneath a bud at the base of the cutting. Place the cuttings the right way up in a shallow trench to which you have added grit or sand. Refill the trench with soil. The cuttings should be 15 cm apart and each cutting should have two buds above the surface. And then wait. When new leaf growth appears you know the cuttings have rooted. Wait until the next autumn and plant out.

   Blackcurrants like full sun but will produce heavy crops in a slightly shady, but not dark, spot. They also like moist soil that doesn't get waterlogged, so it's a case of plenty of muck before planting. Of the several varieties available, the one every plotholder seems to rate is Ben Lomond. It tastes great, is resistant to many diseases, including the dreaded mildew, and is a mid-season fruiting variety. Whichever variety you choose, make sure you protect the plants from the birds. Take care when using netting as saggy or torn netting not only allows birds onto crops, but can also trap them.

I'm on the lookout for some nice blackcurrants to take hardwood cuttings from this autumn.

Joe's Veg Heroes
Toby Buckland

Toby is the lead presenter on *Gardeners' World*, carrying on in the long tradition of accomplished and inspiring gardeners. Toby trained at Cambridge University Botanic Gardens and has presented many gardening shows and written several books. Toby has his own allotment and visited my plot in the summer. He said he was impressed and I believe him!

Toby Buckland

🍃 **Allotment** South Devon

🍃 **Plot size** 8 x 25 metres

🍃 **Annual rent** £15 per year

🍃 **Soil type** silty, neutral to slightly alkaline

🍃 **Biggest growing problem** Not having running water on the site. I have lots of water butts instead, but the real saviours are two jerry cans bought from army surplus and kept in the boot of the car.

🍃 **Favourite tool** There aren't many gardening tasks a spade can't do and although I'm not a tool sentimentalist, one of my favourite things on the allotment is my clockwork radio. It's amazing how much weeding you can get done during a frustrating World Cup campaign.

Favourite crop Aaah, tomatoes. At times like this, when I'm writing in November and they've all been eaten up or killed by the cold, you appreciate their real value. To think just a couple of months ago I had them by the bucketful …

Favourite time of year Harvest-time of course!

What's your first memory of vegetable growing? Gardening in my uncle's veg plot and being told the story of how the family's legacy – a bag of uncut rubies smuggled out of South Africa early last century – was inadvertently thrown on a bonfire and raked out to feed the onions on my grandfather's allotment. It's now a car park and every-time I pass I keep an eye out in case I see something red and shiny glinting from the gutter.

When did you first take on an allotment? I took on my first plot in 1994. I remember thinking 'gosh this is big, and what well-grown couch grass'.

Why do you love the allotment so much? The pleasure of pulling fresh produce from the soil can't be beaten. But more than that, it's the sense of freedom that you get from gardening on an allotment. Where else could you collect broken pallets and make use of an old bathtub without lowering the tone?

What do you do with your excess produce? Swap it with neighbours and freeze as much of the rest as I can in the form of soups.

What's the best advice you can give to other growers? Never stoop and pick up nothing – or never bend down if you're not going to do something useful when you're down there.

Why do you think allotments are so important? They have their own rhythm related to the seasons that's always constant. This makes them stand apart from the commercial clutter and hustle outside the gates.

Autumn veg

Putting in my autumn onions and garlic felt like a significant moment. I had missed the opportunity the year before as I hadn't even found an allotment then, but now it felt as if I was actually up to speed and in sync with everyone else, putting in plants at the correct time. I also potted up some extra onions and garlic so that I had some more as back-up if any failed, but also so they could go into the spaces that would be left when I pulled out the last potatoes and sweet potatoes.

Ken popped by while I was doing this and gave me a huge parsnip which I thought was too big to really taste good. How wrong I was. Cathy made enormous quantities of absolutely delicious soup from this single parsnip. They're one of my favourite veggies and next year I'm definitely going to grow them.

Sow and plant

Although temperatures start to drop in autumn, planting doesn't stop as there are still plenty of crops that can go into the ground whilst the soil is still warm and workable. Some will put on strong root growth during the winter and returns will be better the following spring and summer. Others will crop quickly, providing produce during the leaner early spring period.

Shallots can be planted at this time of year. It's the usual planting technique and I tried a variety called Griselle. It is a favourite of the French who claim it is the most flavoursome shallot you can grow. The bulbs soon multiply, producing many long, grey and yellow-skinned shallots. These can be eaten fresh from the plot in June or stored for a few months. Check your newly-planted shallots every day, as the birds do seem to enjoy pulling them out. If they do, just ease the bulbs back into the soil.

Spring cabbages can also be planted in autumn, and will heart up at the end of spring or in early summer. Like most brassicas, they need fertile soil that's been trampled or firmed down. It's essential to net the young plants at this time of year, because pigeons never seem to rest. Try Primo for a solid head and Savoy King if you fancy a flamboyant Savoy type. I'm told that a variety called Siberia is worth a go, due to its colossal hardiness.

Spinach can be both sown and planted. Sow the seed directly into warm, early autumn soil, 1 cm (0.4 inches) deep with rows 30 cm (12 inches) apart. Make sure you sow plenty because it cooks down to virtually nothing. If you are all sown out by autumn, your local garden centre should have pre-grown spinach seedlings for sale. Sprinkle a handful of fish, blood and bone before planting as spinach is greedy, requires plenty of moisture and plenty of compost in the soil. If your plants survive to summer you will need to provide dappled shade. But spinach really is worth the trouble. I grew two varieties: Medania for it's large round leaves, and Toscane for use as baby spinach leaves.

It's time to put in some hardy peas for an early crop next year. Clear a shallow trench 5 cm (2 inches) deep and the width of your spade. Sow a hardy pea such as Feltham First in two rows along the trench, cover and label. Plants will soon appear, sit happily over winter and produce delicious pods in May. All the support they need is a few twigs pushed in around the plants as they only grow to 45 cm (1.5 feet).

When I first took over the plot I was amazed to see fellow plotholders with tall broad beans smothered in pods. I now know they sow in autumn. The variety everyone seems to use is Aquadulce Claudia. It has an award of garden merit (AGM) from the Royal Horticultural Society so it must be good. Sow in October and strong plants will be formed by winter. They are tough and will start to produce 15 cm (6 inch) long pods filled with tender white broad beans next spring and summer. It is best to net the seedlings, as the shoots are a delicacy to hungry birds.

1 Some people plant supermarket garlic and get good results, but bulbs grown on specifically for planting are certified virus free and should guarantee good results. **2** You can still plant out winter lettuce in the autumn but a cloche will protect them and speed up their growth.

PUMPKINS

I must have been a bit mad, but I planted a donated pumpkin as an afterthought. There was a spare piece of land and Keith had a couple of plants going, which he kindly donated to the Swift allotment fund. Stanley barrowed over a couple of loads of compost, planted them directly into the top of it, and we thought no more about them. Almost overnight the long stems were covering the path and soon the pumpkins started to appear. Then the competition was mentioned. Keith and Manuel were both growing pumpkins to see whose was going to be the heaviest, and they asked me if I'd like to have a go. I responded with a tentative 'Yes'.

I read up on pumpkins and found lots of myth and folklore surrounding their growth. Some growers feed every day with their own concoctions of anything from racehorse or sheep manure steeped in stream water to beer. Others nip off the growing point once three fruits have set and one or two only allow a single fruit to set on each plant. One champion grower bans anyone from walking near his pumpkins so that the delicate feeding roots near the surface of the soil aren't damaged.

I let my pumpkin go free range and 4x4. Naturally, it only produced three pumpkins and one of them was a late developer. However, despite this it did really well in the weigh-in. Keith won the competition with a 38 kilo (84 pound) pumpkin, we came second with 34 kilos and Manuel had 32 kilos, although he said he had one at home over 60 kilos. Yeah, right!

Manuel had grown his on a shed-like roof which I thought made fantastic use of a small area, and I might do the same in the future. Or I might bung a plant in the third bay of my compost heap – the one crammed with compost – and see what happens. I might even get my hands on some manure to top up the compost. It's a traditional method of growing pumpkins – and I might beat Manuel and Keith into the bargain.

Pumpkins do like feed, they do like moisture, they do like sun, and they do like having the fruits lifted off the soil with a brick or straw (this stops them from rotting as the autumn temperatures drop). Never allow the fruits to get frosted, as the flesh will turn to mush. Once cut, you can dry them off in a frost-free shed where they should be safe from mice. I grew Atlantic Giant and loved the enormous orange-skinned fruit. The kids helped me carve it into a fabulous Halloween face, and it felt wonderful growing, eating and carving our own.

···⟩
1 These are my two beauties almost ready for harvesting. **2** Okay Keith, you win! **3** Connie has certainly inherited the creative gene, but said it was a portrait of me! Thanks. **4** Stanley loves barrowing the compost, and he planted the pumpkins directly into a mound of the stuff.

GARLIC

Autumn is a great time to plant garlic, although traditionally gardeners planted garlic on the shortest day and harvested on the longest. I like the idea of warm, moist soil encouraging roots out, a bit of top growth and a great crop early next summer.

Planting garlic is very much like planting onion sets: you dig a small hole and drop in an individual clove, then backfill with soil ensuring the pointy end is uppermost and just covered. Netting will stop birds from being a nuisance.

Ideally, garlic needs well-drained soil. My raised beds were good as they had a high proportion of compost and didn't get waterlogged at all during the year. Add sharp sand to your garlic bed or row before planting if you have a clay soil, which will help with drainage. They also need the sunniest position you have, so avoid planting large, leafy crops nearby. It's also best to avoid planting in soil where you have recently added fresh manure. This can cause the garlic to rot.

I had a bit of a discussion with the other plot holders about whether or not you can plant leftover 'ordinary' supermarket garlic. I thought it would be cheaper (it's already been bought and is going to waste) than buying cloves via mail order or the garden centre. However, when I looked into it I discovered it is best not to use leftovers. The supermarket stuff could well be imported from far-flung places and not really be suitable for UK conditions. It might also have been treated with any number of chemicals to stop it from growing, and it could even be carrying viral problems – which you would only find out once the plants are growing. Mail order it was then.

There are now a few different varieties on offer, and I grew Solent Wight, which produces large bulbs that can be stored for months and has a good depth of flavour, and Moldovan Purple, which is a bit of a trendy choice, I admit, but the flavour is sublime and the cloves are easy to peel. I also grew Elephant garlic. Before you write in to complain, I know it isn't true garlic and is actually closer to leeks, but I class it as my all-time favourite garlic. It is *the* choice if you like roasting garlic. The bulbs grow to the size of a cricket ball and the flowering heads can reach 1 metre (3.3 feet) high. If flowering heads are produced, just snap them off as you want every bit of energy put into bulb production. It's great on the plot, but I reckon it is just as good in a garden border.

Autumn-planted garlic is ready the following summer and can be harvested when the leaves turn yellow. Once you've been given the signal, you just ease the bulbs out of the soil with a fork, loosen any soil around the roots and spread them out in the sun to dry. Keith had a really great display of drying garlic on the one sunny week of last summer. Ideally you want the air to get all around the bulbs, so put them on a wire net. Storage is simple enough: either put them in a net bag or plait them together.

Rust is a problem (see page 135), but I had a real fright with a more deadly and long-lasting disease. White rot can decimate all garlic, onions and the rest of the onion family. The symptoms are yellowing leaves and, most importantly, fluffy white growths on the bulbs. One morning, just before the film crew arrived, I noticed the leaves of each and every one of my garlic plants were looking yellow, and at the side of one bulb a white mould had developed. I consulted other plot holders who seemed nonplussed by it, so in mounting fear I reached for some books, but it turned out to be simply a bit of mould from the compost and the start of rust.

If you really do have white rot you can't grow onions in that area for at least eight years. I've never been so pleased to have rust diagnosed.

SOWING GARLIC
1 Split each bulb into cloves and as always check they are nice and firm. **2** Plant the garlic approximately 3 cm (1.2 inches) deep so the pointy tip is just below the soil level and firm in the soil around it.

JAPANESE ONIONS

This is the time of year to get ahead of the game and put in some onions for the following summer. They aren't maincrop varieties, but something labelled Japanese or overwintering onions. The idea is that these specially bred varieties will provide you with an earlier crop than your usual maincrops. Expect to be eating this lot in June and July. So, if you like your onions (and we do), they are an essential part of a plot plan.

Ken showed me his way of planting overwintering onion sets and, judging by the ones on his plot, I'm not going to argue with his method. He recommends that, instead of making a drill or individual holes for the sets, you create a ridge and plant the sets into this. The theory is that water drains away from the base of the set and encourages good root formation. By planting in autumn the sets get a chance to develop a root system and a few shoots before winter hits. But even in a cold winter the root system can be slowly developing, so that with the onset of spring, they are off to a flying start.

You don't want to plant too early in autumn as this might give the sets too much time to produce leaf growth which could get damaged by a hard winter. Ideally, by the end of autumn you want each plant to have three or four shoots, then you can let the roots get on with it. So, as a rough rule of thumb, plant overwintering onion sets around the time of the first frosts.

I grew three varieties of overwintering sets, including Radar, which are a nice traditional onion shape and tasty. I planted them 15 cm (6 inches) apart and netted them to stop the birds pulling out the strawy tips. I also planted Electric, which is a stunning, hardy red onion that grows away quickly in spring to produce a crop in June; and Senshyu Yellow, which is one of the first overwintering onions that was available to amateurs to grow and produces flat-bottomed onions with browny-yellow skin. A fellow plot holder has suggested a British-bred variety called Shakespeare. It produces bulbs with darker brown skin than most and has fantastic keeping qualities. I'm beginning to wonder whether one plot is enough.

Planting at this time of year does present the veg gardener with a problem. Or to be more positive, an opportunity to get rid of some mice. They can be quite active in winter and will have a nibble at your overwintering onion sets. There are many ways to get rid of or deter mice, but a humane trap-and-release at a safe distance, is my preferred method. Traps that kill often only maim and poisons are a no-no for me and the family.

SOWING ONIONS
1 Check each set to make sure it isn't rotten and 'has enough meat in it', as Ken says. 2 I find it's sometimes quicker and easier to dig a shallow trench with a hand trowel along the edge of a board rather than planting each set individually. 3 Space the sets about 15 cm (6inches) apart and nuzzle them in to the trench. 4 Cover with soil just to the level of the tips.

Seasonal problems

Mice

At this time of year the mice are beginning to come back in from the fields and wherever else they scurry about during the summer months, to find warmer places for the cold winter season. And one of the warmest places on an allotment is a compost heap. It can be quite alarming forking over your compost bin to unearth a nest of mice.

Mice will feast on all kinds of crops, especially broad beans and peas, which they can devour in the spring before they've even had a chance to grow. They'll also wreak havoc with any stored veg in the shed, so you don't want to leave them loitering in your compost bins over the winter.

Mice will be attracted by the warmth and dryness of the heap. If you're afraid or disinclined to remove them manually, you can try to dissuade their continued presence by disturbing their peace and quiet and literally bullying them out of their new home.

Try soaking your compost heap with water from a hosepipe. Saturate its contents and then turn it all over. You should be doing this turning process as a matter of course to increase the speed of composting anyway. Then, before it dries out again, give it another good soaking. After three of these soak and turn episodes, the mice should be sufficiently deterred from making a comeback. Of course, they will have moved somewhere else, possibly nibbling the seed packets in your shed, but at least you won't jump back in shock at discovering them in your heap next time around.

One word of warning – always wear gloves when flooding and turning your heap. Mice have weak bladders and you don't want to be handling their waste.

Mildew

It may well be the time of gorgeous leaf colour, scrunching leaves, collecting conkers and smoky bonfires, but mildew on your crops is a sure sign that autumn has hit the plot. It can start in the summer, but in the autumn it tends to see off those few crops that are trying their best to produce something late on. Both powdery and downy mildew can affect most vegetables at some stage.

Courgettes are particularly prone to being brought down by mildew attacks, and part of the reason is the nature of their growth. To get a hold, airborne mildew spores need stagnant air. The closely bunched, tangled stems of courgettes trap still air to provide almost perfect conditions for mildew. Add to this the way water can collect on their mat of leaves during rain or watering and it's little wonder the leaves quickly become covered in a white powdery coat.

Mildew can attack in summer when the plant's natural defence systems are under the stress of coping with the dry conditions, but October is the usual mildew season. The disease cripples plants as leaves cannot function and quickly die.

The good news is that different plants suffer from different mildews. In other words, your roses are safe from your courgette mildew. The bad news is that mildews often successfully lurk on weeds before infecting your plants, so you have to keep those edges clean and tidy.

Now, sprays. You can get sprays to use against powdery mildew, but these must be used with great care and it is essential to read the labels. Despite the robust nature of even an ailing courgette plant, many chemicals easily damage the leaves.

The chemical that does most damage to mildews is sulphur, and sulphur powders are available to allotmenteers and gardeners. I didn't and don't want to use anything chemical on my crops, so next year I will try to grow my plants better.

A few pointers gleaned from fellow plot holders who have had to overcome the problem for years are:

- Never let the plants become stressed by water shortages.
- When watering, take extra time and make sure you water the roots and don't simply flick the water over the leaves.
- Remove any leaf that becomes yellow or sickly, and even take away healthy leaves that are causing congestion. This improves airflow around the plants.
- Don't use fertilizers around plants as this produces lush growth that is easily infected. Grow your plants hard.
- Don't expect a plant to adapt to your conditions. If a plant needs a sunny site, give it a sunny site. Likewise, shade lovers will be stressed by full sun.
- When choosing your seed, look out for mildew-resistant varieties.

I've talked with a number of my fellow plot holders about the problem and a couple of them told me about a method for preventing mildew that they had read about on the internet. I know it might not be the best recommendation, but it might be worth a try – not that I have tried it or even recommend it (those lawyers again).

The idea is that you dilute milk with water (one part milk, nine parts water) and use the mixture as a spray to help the fight against mildew. The theory behind it is that the milk, which is alkaline, neutralizes the acidity on the leaves and stops the spores from growing. Like I said, I haven't tried it, but it seems to be working for someone out there.

1 The wet summer caused rather unsightly mildew on my courgettes. The good news is that it didn't affect the crop in any way and they can still be eaten and taste just the same.
2 Mice have had a good nibble of this tomato.

Essential kit for your allotment

There are a few things that are optional extras for an allotment site, but once you've got them, you'll wonder how you ever lived without them. (I'd actually argue that they are essential extras…)

Three bins for three reasons

You can't say your allotment is functioning correctly until you have a few compost bins, or heaps, and the cheaper they are to produce the better. I built mine in early spring when I wanted a job to do while the soil was too wet to work, but if you haven't got one by autumn, you'll need to get on with it. Sure, you can buy plastic Dalek types, but they never have enough capacity for an abundant plot. Anything else is usually too expensive to risk on an open site. Enter stage left: pallets.

Good old pallets. Non-returnable and completely above-board pallets, of course, they are the ones readily available from merchants around the country. Keith gave me a tip off about a local merchant who traded in new and used pallets. It was only a mile or so away and the film crew had the van. Perfect. I loaded the van with pallets and back at the plot set about making compost bins. I had the space and enough pallets to make three large bins. If you can, make the bins around pallet-sized cubes; anything more and the contents can struggle to heat up, and anything less will simply fill up too quickly. The bins aren't hard to make – simply nail pallets together to create cubes.

Positioning the bins is often dictated by the plot geography. Mine are behind the shed, at the back of the plot, next to a path and slightly hidden from view. Perfect. I can get to them easily and they aren't an eyesore (not that a compost bin should be deemed an eyesore – they are, after all, the heartbeat of your soil).

I erected my bins on bare soil. This is important as it allows free movement of organisms from the soil into the compost, which is vital if you want all your organic waste to break down. Some plot holders actually construct their bins over a pit; this increases the volume of the bin and ensures a close relationship between soil and compost.

I made three bins as I wanted one to be used for making compost, the second to store made compost and the third to store council compost.

The ideal situation is that one bin is always making compost, and this is the one you should add all your waste to, while the second bin should be full and cooking on full heat; this is the one you use when home-made compost crops up in the recipe. My third bin is the one in which I keep the free council compost, but sometimes that compost needed a few more weeks of cooking, and my bin gave it that chance.

Researching compost made me realize that more has been written and spoken about composting than any other subject. Everyone seems to have his or her own recipe, technique and tips to make perfect compost. My top ten tips for better compost are:

1 I throw almost all my vegetative waste onto my compost heap, and next year will have plenty of my own to put back into the soil. **2** The waste quickly heats up and breaks down to form compost. When it gets to this crumbly texture it's ready to use. I stockpiled plenty of the council stuff in one of my bins.

🍃 Line the compost bins with cardboard. This acts as insulation, keeps the temperature high and eventually rots down, adding valuable carbon to the mix.

🍃 Cover the heap to prevent waterlogging and to keep heat in.

🍃 Turn the heap. This means getting the whole contents of the bin out, giving it a good old mix and putting it back again. It prevents stagnant layers developing. You need to do this twice a year.

1

2

🍃 Water the heap if it is too dry – you can tell if this is the case as it will be dusty and nothing will rot down.

🍃 Ensure you have a mix of nitrogen-rich waste and carbon-rich waste – too much of either will result in poor compost. Grass cuttings and soft stems are rich in nitrogen, while cardboard and paper is rich in carbon. An equal mix of nitrogen and carbon, or at least a third nitrogen, is ideal.

🍃 Shred the material before you put it into the heap, as this increases the surface area that the bacteria and fungi have to work on.

🍃 Add a spadeful of your plot's soil to the mix to generate plenty of bacterial and fungal activity.

🍃 Add comfrey leaves to the mix for a real boost. Don't bother with other expensive compost activators – a good heap doesn't need them.

🍃 Make as many bins as you have the space or cash for. An allotment is generous with its compost material and opportunities for free garden waste (collected leaves from the council in autumn) abound.

🍃 Be patient – compost from compost bins can take a year to mature and be ready for use.

1 Old (free!) pallets are ideal for building compost heaps. For the outer edges I infilled the gaps between the boards with offcuts to keep the heat in. **2** Rustic carpentry! I nailed the whole construction together using galvanized nails. **3** It's important to turn the compost with a fork at least twice a year.

What to put in your heap is also a rich vein of discussion at our site, and no doubt sites across the country. Stick to this list and you won't go far wrong:

PUT THESE IN YOUR HEAP	KEEP THESE OUT OF YOUR HEAP
Grass cuttings	Meat
Vegetable peelings	Dairy products
Shredded woody plants	Animal waste
Teabags	Diseased plants
Old flowers	Perennial weeds (such as horsetail)
Annual weeds	Any cooked food
All spent bedding plants	
Coffee grounds	
Cardboard	
Egg boxes	
Scrunched up newspaper	
Shredded bills and letters	
Leaves	
Sawdust	
Eggshells	

You know the compost is ready to use when it smells earthy, is crumbly and is dark brown in colour. Use it wherever you need – to line trenches, as mulch, or just to dig in to improve the plot.

Green manure

It may sound like something you get from sick animals, but no, green manure is a genuinely pleasant topic to talk about on your plot or over the dinner table. Green manure is a fast-growing crop that you sow into vacant soil. A crop of green manure will:

- Suppress weed growth.
- Stop winter rain from washing nutrients out of the range of roots.
- Provide a green crop to dig into the soil.
- Provide a green crop that can be harvested and added to compost.

Urban Farmer Joe! I sowed Hungarian grazing rye in the autumn as it's a good all-rounder and will help keep my claggy soil open and improve drainage.

In other words, it improves the soil – and that can't be bad when you have a heavy clay soil like mine (it also adds bulk to thin sandy soils). There are different types of green manure and you can get the seeds from garden centres or by mail order. The autumn is a great time to be sowing green manure, mainly because the soil is warm enough to get the seeds growing and it's the time when a bit of soil is often free of crops. The main types are:

TYPE	SOW	GROWS	SOIL TYPE	NITROGEN FIXER	BEAR IN MIND
Winter tares	Summer and Autumn	Over winter	Clay	Yes	Good for all areas
Hungarian grazing rye	Autumn	Autumn and spring	All	No	Great all-rounder
Field beans	Autumn	Over winter	Clay	Yes	Dig in before flowers appear
Buckwheat	Spring and summer	Up to autumn	All	No	Tolerates poor soils
Phacelia	Summer	Up to autumn, again in spring	Lighter Soils	No	Only for milder areas
Red clover	Early summer	Most of the year	No acid soils	Yes	Cut early to avoid flowers
Mustard	Spring to autumn	Two months after sowing	All	No	Quick crop when soil becomes vacant

Whatever green manure you use, always wait a month between digging it into the soil and planting up with your vegetables. Some of the roots of the green manure contain germination inhibitors that will stop seeds growing. Never dig the green manure crop in deeply – all that is required is a quick flick of the spade and it's there in the root zone. It may be useful to chop the tougher stalks before digging in, as this will help the stalks to break down.

Water butts

My shed might not win any beauty contests, but it is useful. One obvious benefit is storage; providing shelter from the rain is another; but aiding water collection is the best.

The place where I got the pallets for the compost bins also sold old containers. The ones I got, for a couple of quid each, were used as orange juice concentrate containers. I bought three and got them back to the plot. And that's when the discussions began. One water butt was never going to be enough, and after rigging up guttering and a downpipe into the first, thoughts turned to linking up butts two and three. I thought it would be simple, but Keith, with his keen engineering brain, soon threw a spanner in the works by suggesting there were two different options for linking them together to ensure that all three of them would eventually fill up. But which would be the best?

Option one was to connect the three butts near the top. The idea was that when the rainwater had filled the first and reached the interconnecting pipe, the water would overflow into the second butt, and then when the water had filled the second, it would overflow into the third. This system would require a tap at the base of each butt. Nice and easy.

Option two was to connect the three butts near the bases of each. Water would then fill up the first butt to this low pipe and then overflow into the

It may look a bit Heath Robinson, but my system of water butts certainly work well enough and after a heavy downpour they fill up surprisingly quickly.

second. The same thing would happen again into the third butt. In this system the water is level in each of the three butts at any one point in time. This system would need only one tap at the base of the first butt.

We managed to debate this for a good couple of hours before I decided, for no particular reason except to stop the debate, that I was going to connect the water butts at the top with taps at the base of each. Done. I also made sure the water butts were high enough off the ground to get a watering can underneath the taps, so I placed them on a few pallets.

It only took one rainy day to fill the first butt and the second was soon called into action. I did make a mistake in buying opaque water butts – the water quickly turned green and I imagine if I didn't use it quickly the algae would cause problems blocking the taps. I could paint them black or cover them, or wait until the merchant has some large black containers in stock and buy those as replacements.

1 I covered the roof with some plastic sheeting pinned down at the edges to stop any leaks and to ensure all the rainwater goes into the gutter and into the down pipe. **2** The butts are raised off the ground on pallets so that I can get my watering can under the tap.

1

2

Storing veg

However you grow your veg, there will be times when you have too much of one crop. It's inevitable, as even successional sowing doesn't stop one courgette plant producing loads of fruit, and your maincrop onions generally do all go in and come out at the same time. But in the deep winter you and the family will be only too glad of some stored veg.

Blanching and freezing

The best way to store veg is in the freezer. I know it uses electricity, but to avoid mouldy, shrivelled specimens it is the only way. The trick with freezing any veg is blanching. This is a process that involves killing the enzyme activity in the veg before super-cooling it. In other words, you kill the veg to stop it going off and losing its taste. The way to do this is to cut your veg (courgettes, for example, should ideally be sliced), and plunge them into boiling water. Allow the water to come back to the boil and keep the veg in there, being bullied by the bubbles, for a few minutes. Next you need to super-cool the blanched veg by putting it into a bowl of cold water (ice-cube cold if you can), before patting it dry and packing it. This way the enzymes are stopped in their tracks and the nutritional value of the veg is maintained. Repeat the same process for runner beans.

A lot of veg (cauliflowers, Brussels sprouts, fennel and peppers) are best blanched in boiling water for three minutes. Other veg can take less time: French beans, shredded cabbage, parsnips and peas; whilst others take a little longer. Aubergines, for example, take four minutes, a good solid beetroot about five, and large sweetcorn takes eight minutes. It's also best to blanch in small portions, as that way you ensure the quality of blanch.

Once you have blanched your veggies and have cooled them as described above, drain them well and then put them straight into freezer bags or airtight containers and place them in the freezer.

Storing onions

Right, now for that mountain of onions. They aren't too good bunged in the freezer, as they thaw out to a mushy mess and are tasteless to boot. The best way to keep them is to rope or string them together à la stereotypical French cyclist. However, a cool, dry store is better than handlebars any jour of the semaine. There is a real skill in stringing onions together, and you can expect to have a few bouncing on the floor as you perfect the technique.

There are three main points to adhere to when storing onions, and in fact all vegetables:

◗ The veg should be dried before storage. This will reduce the amount of spoilage.

◗ The veg should be sound, i.e. not diseased or damaged in any way. Bruised veg will rot in store so use it immediately.

STRINGING FOR BEGINNERS

I learnt this technique off a plot holder who grows thousands of onions a year. His shed is a picture. Give it a go; keep your temper and practise patience. Oh, and hang the working string from a good height to avoid unnecessary back strain.

◗ Cut a 2 metre (6.6 inches) length of strong string or rope.

◗ Fold it in half.

◗ Twist the ends together to form a loop.

◗ Put the neck of a dried onion in that loop.

◗ Tighten the loop around it.

◗ Weave the stem of a second onion around the string.

◗ Push the onion downwards onto the first onion.

◗ Weave the stem of the third onion around the string in the opposite direction to the second.

◗ Push this onion down.

◗ Carry on with this alternate weaving until you have a long string of onions, and one you can easily lift.

There. Nothing to it. Or if that is too much hassle, put dried-off onions into wooden trays in a cool, dry place.

I got a really good crop of onions and shallots in my first year. After drying out they go into my cool dry cellar where they last for absolutely ages.

DRYING OFF

Onions should be dried off on the soil but in the sun for a week or so before storing. Placing them on mesh, held above the soil by small stakes, is ideal, covering them if it rains. This hardens the skins and helps the onions last longer in store.

Potatoes should have 'hard' skin before storage to reduce rotting. Leave them on the soil surface for a few hours before storing, but don't leave them too long as the potatoes will turn green and will cause stomach upsets if eaten.

Clamp it

This is an old-fashioned way to store some kinds of veg. Carrots, potatoes, beetroot, swede and celeriac can all be clamped – and as long as your plot isn't overrun with rodents – it really works. The principle behind it is to keep frost away from your stored veg. You do this by using straw (an excellent insulator, and cheap to buy, too) and soil. The veg doesn't rot as it is in contact with straw – the soil keeps the whole thing surprisingly dry. A vent at the top allows air circulation – and of course you keep checking for the odd rogue rotter.

- Choose a dry spot, about 1.2 m/4 feet in diameter, where water doesn't collect.
- Dig a trench a spade's width around the clamp site to help with drainage, and save the soil.
- Place a 5 cm/2 inch layer of straw on the soil.
- Nuzzle a layer of your crop, for example carrots, onto the straw in a circle, with the thick ends of the carrots pointing towards the outside.
- Add another layer of straw.
- Then add a smaller layer of the crop.
- Then more straw.
- And then …you get the picture.
- Eventually you'll have created a cone-shaped mound of vegetables and straw. Pull a tuft of straw out of the top to act as a chimney for moisture.
- Pat a 5 cm/2 inch layer of soil over the clamp, and there you have it. Snug as a bug in a rug, and ready for you whenever you get the urge for a carrot. You should regularly check your clamp for signs of damage or mice.

1 Sow green manure such as this Hungarian rye in early autumn, whilst the soil is still warm enough to ensure good germination. **2** Dry and store some beans for planting out next spring, but only if the plants they grew on were disease-free.

DO'S AND DON'TS OF STORAGE

📎 Do try to store as much as possible, as you will be thankful for your efforts in the middle of winter.

📎 Do use anything immediately that you suspect is 'going off' or rotting.

📎 Don't store in temperatures that fluctuate – the roof space of your home, for example, may seem cool but a little sun can quickly heat it up.

📎 Don't store in places where mice and other vermin may be present.

PLOT ESSENTIALS – AUTUMN

If you have one day a week at the plot, make sure you:

📎 Set up a compost heap.

📎 Clear away crops as they die.

📎 Harvest everything and store surplus crops.

📎 Sow green manure seeds in vacant soil.

Joe's Veg Heroes
Terry Walton

Terry Walton is the complete organic allotment hero. He got his first plot in 1957 at 11 years of age. He has a regular slot on Jeremy Vine's BBC Radio 2 show, and when he isn't on his allotment he gives talks and also writes. I first heard him on the radio reporting direct from his allotment on his mobile phone and after a search managed to get his number.

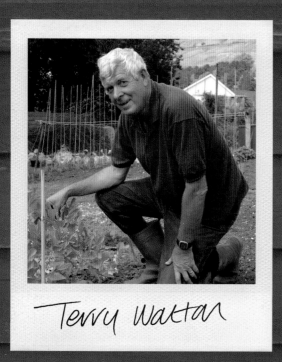

Terry Walton

Allotment The Partridge Road Allotment Society, Llwynypia, Rhondda, Wales.

Plot size Currently one plot (once had a total of ten plots in the early 1960s), with one shed and a greenhouse.

Annual rent £14 per year.

Soil type Acid clay.

Biggest growing problem Club root. It's been in the soil forever and we'll never get rid of it. I grow brassicas on in 12 cm/5 inch pots, dig a 30 cm/12 inch hole for each one and lime both the ground and the hole and pack in fresh compost every time. It does the trick.

Favourite tool Dutch hoe.

Favourite crop I've got two. Peas, as I love to pop them and eat them instantly, but it means they rarely make it to the kitchen. I love runner beans as they take up little ground space, crop prolifically, and store well. Nothing tastes better than the first handful of the year with a knob of butter.

🫛 **Favourite time of year** The autumn, as you can look back at the year, look at your full shed store and see what you've achieved. There's nothing better than the soil damp with dew, some hazy autumn sunshine and the chance to sit back and reflect.

🫛 **What's your first memory of vegetable growing?** Going for the first time with my father as a four-year-old to his allotment. He was holding my hand tightly. It was inhabited only by men; all smartly dressed with shirts, ties and flat caps. I went to pick some blackcurrants off a large bush, but was immediately told off by Alf Daniels. I'll never forget it.

🫛 **When did you first take on an allotment?** I took over my first allotment aged 11, which was a major breakthrough in its time as all the others were taken by older men. Looking back, it probably had something to do with my father being on the committee. My first plot was at the farthest top corner, which is the poorest part of the site where all newcomers start; they work their way down to nearer the gate and I'm now currently at number two.

🫛 **Why do you love the allotment so much?** It's a mixture of things really. The healthy fresh air, the exercise, the social life, and it's a relaxing place to be. Eating fresh produce within hours of harvesting is the best way. You have the complete freedom to grow what you want, and if you're ever short your neighbours will always help you out. I spend 4–5 hours a day on my allotment, 7 days a week, but these days there's plenty of relaxing and socialising. The gang put the world to rights and pick the Welsh football and rugby teams.

🫛 **What do you do with your excess produce?** We share what we have on the plot and nothing goes to waste. We store, freeze, and my wife makes preserves. She can also work miracles with courgettes, which is just as well as we always have so many!

🫛 **What's the best advice you can give to other growers?** There are two. There's a way to tie runner bean sticks together so they're bonded together and wind-proof even if some of the string snaps. And how to make a smelly rhubarb soup by soaking rhubarb leaves for about 5 weeks in an old dustbin. I use it neat to feed the brassicas and it keeps the cabbage whites off too. It really works!

🫛 **What would be your best piece of advice to other growers?** Always start out slowly and deal with one bit at a time, but make sure you get something back out of it too. It's easy to work really hard, but not get any rewards, which is demoralising and will make you feel as if you're going nowhere.

Winter at the Plot

It's strange; having gardened in the UK for many years I have a real love/
hate relationship with our winters. Although recent ones have been pretty
mild, I've found the leaves do always fall off the trees eventually and other
plants become dormant and stop growing, even if it's only for a short while.
This means that, as a garden designer, I've found that no-one is in a rush
to have their garden designed and bulit, and as a TV presenter there's little
to film during the winter months as mud and twigs, however beautiful,
are rarely the best subject matter. The positive side of all this is that I can
actually start to dictate the pace of my own life for a short while, which
I really look forward to.

The negative side, however, is that after the beauty of autumn, I find
winter can be depressing in a wet, grey London. I'm fine up until about
Christmas time, but it's the slow months of January, February and March –
around a quarter of the year – that tend to drag. Last winter did feel very
different, though, as I had the allotment to focus on and get me through.
It hasn't miraculously changed the way I feel about those months, but
it has certainly given me a focus, diverted my attention, and made spring
even more eagerly anticipated.

Cold, dark days of winter are the ideal time to start planning for
the next year. By my bed and in the bathroom, where there were once
magazines and the odd Arsenal programme to read, fruit and veg seed
catalogues have been starting to take over! Now I never thought I'd turn
into 'one of those', but somehow it happened. It'll be a flat cap next …

I've started to work out where to put in my crops to keep the rotation
going and also thought about how to make the whole plot much more
productive. My first year had been all about getting the allotment up and
running and getting to grips with the basics, but now I wanted to start
using the space as efficiently as possible too. This is where looking at other
people's plots really helps, as you can see how plants actually grow, how
much space they take up and how long they take to produce.

Some plants, such as onions, garlic, brassicas, potatoes, etc., are what
I call 'slow burners' and need a long time in the ground. I had put all my
onions, garlic and shallots into a precious diamond, but next year this'll
be where I grow all the sprinter crops, such as salads, herbs, etc.

Winter jobs

Winter gave me the opportunity to get stuck in to some other projects too. After my 'allotment envy' in the summer I decided my plot needed more tall structures on it to grow peas and beans, but also to grow squashes and pumpkins, taking a leaf out of Manuel's book. Winter is the ideal time to do this sort of heavy manual work, as it keeps you warm.

Any old materials will do for construction – old bits of wood or metal that have been obtained by the frugal allotment philosophy of paying as little as possible, or ideally nothing, for the materials. Skips become a very useful source of materials, and the palette company just round the corner is always looking to get rid of anything it can't sell on.

There was also some major digging to be done.

Pea and bean trench recipe

The quieter months over winter are the ideal time to start planning for the year to come. If you want hassle-free peas and beans, now is a good time to sort out the soil. I stumbled across a great recipe for a pea and bean trench, which I used in spring, but winter is the ideal time to get it sorted. I followed this recipe and didn't need to water my peas and beans throughout the year, and the crops were fantastic. It's a great way to sort out a heavy clay soil for future crops.

Dig out a trench a couple of spade widths wide and half a metre deep. Line the trench with cardboard or scrunched up newspaper. Water the cardboard and newspaper before adding anything else. Throw in a load of grass clippings, and on top of that put in as much vegetable material as you have spare. Sprinkle on a generous handful or two of fish, blood and bone, and top up with the soil. It really is an underground compost heap, and over winter and early spring everything rots down to a lovely texture capable of holding moisture and nutrients around the roots of hungry and thirsty peas and beans.

...⟶
**PREPARING BEAN
AND PEA TRENCHES**
1 Dig out a trench two spades wide by about 50 cm (1.6 feet) deep. **2** Line the bottom with old cardboard. **3** Chuck in old newspaper that's been soaked in a bucket. **4** Add some grass clippings and old vegetable material. **5** Rake to even out. **6** Backfill the old soil mixed with some good compost and some fish, blood and bone.

Creating permanent beds

The great thing about my plot has been that there is plenty of space to play with. Crop rotation keeps everything on its toes, but there are a couple of crops that, once planted, stay there for life. As they are permanent crops they stay in beds that are outside of any rotation system you devise, but because they are long lived, the beds need careful preparation and care.

ASPARAGUS

Monty loved his asparagus at Berryfields, Keith constructed a raised bed devoted to asparagus, and everyone else who loves the crop swears that self-grown asparagus tastes so much better than shop-bought. The crop needs a sheltered but sunny site. It is important to avoid frost pockets because the tender spears you harvest in early spring are the very shoots that get damaged by frost. Wind can also snap off the feathery foliage later in the year; if this happens the crowns never bulk up and yields will be poor.

One of the best ways to grow asparagus is to buy two-year-old asparagus roots, known as 'crowns', from the garden centre. This is quicker than raising asparagus from seed, and crowns are cheaper than pot-grown plants.

To get the best out of your crop, you need to prepare the soil well to begin with:

🌿 Dig out a trench about 15 cm/6 inches deep and mound up a ridge in its centre. Spread out the roots of your crowns over the ridge and carefully fill in the trench with a soil and grit mix. It is an expensive start to the life of the asparagus, but remember it is in there for decades. The roots easily break and dry out if there is any delay in planting, so wrap them in soggy newspaper. Crowns are quicker at producing a crop than seeds, and are also cheaper than pot-grown plants at garden centres.

🌿 Cover with this gritty mix so that the top of the crown is 10 cm/4 inches below the surface of the soil.

🌿 Keep well watered.

🌿 Use a thick layer of compost as mulch in early spring to protect the emerging spears.

🌿 Do not pick the spears in the first year.

🌿 When the feathery foliage dies down in autumn, cut it down to the base and put it on the compost heap.

🌿 Hand-weed and mulch again.

Next comes patience: you will get nothing in the first year, a few spears in the second and then take what you want for a six-week period in the third

My raised beds are permanent although I rotate the crops I grow in them. Next year I want to build on my permanent planting by growing asparagus and rhubarb.

year. It's important to take all the spears in that third year as this helps stimulate more buds to grow from the crown, making the plant stronger. Only crop for that six-week period or you will exhaust the plant.

It is a crop for the long term. There is a lot of faffing around involved, but I am told that the crop when harvested is superb. And most of us have space on our plots for a few metres of asparagus.

Try the variety Gijnlim for early and consistently heavy crops of succulent spears from year three. It's also an all-male variety, which means that its energies are put into spear production rather than seeds, and self-sown seedlings are not a problem.

RHUBARB

Rhubarb is yet another family favourite and a stalwart of the majority of plots I have seen. Surely it is one of the easiest crops to grow. Rhubarb likes well-drained soil, packed with compost, and a sunny position. The corner of one of my diamonds is ideal.

The best way to buy rhubarb is as a dormant crown. You see these in garden centres throughout winter and spring. Plant it up early to ensure the crown doesn't dry out. To get the crown growing it needs to be exposed to cold weather, making planting in late autumn or winter ideal.

🌿 Add plenty of compost to the soil.

🌿 Dig a large hole and place the crown in it, making sure the dormant buds are just above soil level.

🌿 Backfill with a mix of soil, compost and muck.

It is tempting to try to get a few sticks of rhubarb in the first spring after planting. Resist. Rather like asparagus, you need to allow the plant time to bulk up. Year two is fine to take a few sticks. These are better, or tastier, if forced. This is easy enough to do, it just means putting a cover over the plant to force the shoots into elongated growth. The toxic leaves are small and underdeveloped, whereas the tasty stalks are crisp and succulent. You can use posh and expensive terracotta rhubarb forcers, but a bucket or plastic pot weighed down with a large stone does the trick for plot holders on our site. This forcing process can be accelerated by mounding fresh muck around the bucket, which increases the heat and therefore the activity within the bucket.

You should stop picking rhubarb after midsummer for two reasons: the first is that the stems get a bit tough; the second that it gives the plant a chance to bulk up again.

After a few years you will notice the centre of your rhubarb looking bare, with stronger shoots towards the outer part of the clump. This is the time to dig the whole lot up, in early winter, and slice through the crown with your spade. Each young slice should have a few dormant buds and a healthy wad of roots. Throw the balding centre section away and replant the fresh sections to allow the whole process to start again.

There are quite a few varieties available but I am going to stick with two tried and tested types: the consistent Timperley Early with thick and tasty stems, and Prince Albert, for it's exceptionally long stalks.

Rhubarb is my kind of allotment plant as it's so simple to grow. Once in the ground it will keep producing for years to come.

Cold frame

I might not (do not!) have a greenhouse but until I get one to fulfil my dreams, I'm going to sort out a cold frame or two. You can regard a cold frame as either a small, unheated greenhouse or a large cloche.

Cold frames are useful because they act as a halfway house between the snug conditions of a propagator or windowsill and the rough outdoor conditions of the plot. You can use them to harden off seedlings before planting out, as a home for pot-grown seedlings that are tough but need protecting from the harshest winters, or even to grow crops of early carrots. Cold frames really come into their own in late spring when hardening off seedlings, as they will save you the time and mess of having seedlings all over your house and taking them outside every day!

Obviously you can buy ready-made cold frames, but good ones – and that means a frame with a good height – can be expensive. The height is important as it allows taller plants to be sited in the frame and the larger the area the more constant the temperature. It goes without saying that small areas heat up and cool down more rapidly, and most plants like a more even temperature.

So save yourself the expense because, like everything on the allotment, making one cheaply is easy. Using old window frames fished out of skips (with the skip holder's permission, of course), is a traditional way to construct a cold frame. One plot holder told me that a local window replacement company would almost pay him to take a few old windows away, as it saves them time and money trying to dispose of them.

I also rather liked the idea I saw on one plot of utilising straw bales to construct a frame. Four bales were placed in a square as the walls of the cold frame and an old window was placed on top as the lid. The nice thing is that the bales can be stacked on top of each other to raise the height of the walls if you do want to store taller plants at a later date. Bales cost a couple of quid each, the window frame is free, and your seedlings are protected on all sides by a top insulating material. It's another great green option, too, as once the bales get tatty you can compost them or spread them out and use them as pathways, or to lift developing fruit or veg from the soil surface, such as strawberries and pumpkins. One word of warning, though (which might seem obvious but I have to say it anyway): don't use a heater in this frame as you might just set the whole thing alight.

···⊱
**CONSTRUCTING
A COLD FRAME**
1 I used the straw bales left over from Potato Day to make the walls of my cold frame. They're great for insulation and go together like giant lego. **2** I got this old window from a friend and it fitted like a glove. **3** Pots of seedlings can be grown on and protected from frosts. **4** Don't forget to water regularly otherwise the pots will quickly dry out.

Winter sowing and planting

Seeds will not grow in the cold, and usually wet, outdoor conditions found in winter, so it's time to get sowing indoors.

Lots of seeds can be sown indoors – all brassicas, leeks, onions, spinach, turnips, and maincrop peas – and you can now get propagators which will fit on the average windowsill. The individual cells or compartments are ideal for starting off your brassicas, beans and onion sets, but seedlings can become drawn and pale on windowsills, as this is where they compete for the little available light. You can counteract by making full use of the light you've got: a board painted white or covered in tin foil will reflect light back onto seedlings.

Better still, invest in a small grow-house structure. These are cheap and widely available. You can usually fit ten or fifteen seed trays and a few pots inside, and there's room for a small heater to keep frost off your seedlings and temperatures at a comfortable level. Remember to weigh down the base of such structures with paving slabs or bags of sand, as even when fully loaded they can blow over, destroying weeks of growth.

Ideally you would do all this in a greenhouse, if you have one. I haven't, but if I did the growing season would be extended at both ends of the year. Maybe one day …

1 Brussels are good winter fodder but will need staking and yes, netting too, as food is scarce for the birds and a hungry flock will demolish them in no time. **2** Ideally, harvest your parsnips after a hard frost as the starch will turn to sugar and they'll taste sweeter.

Winter harvesting

There are some traditional winter crops I love, and Brussels sprouts and parsnips are among them. Both taste better after a few frosts have sweetened them up, and both are harvested in midwinter.

BRUSSELS SPROUTS

Brussels sprouts are a slow-growing crop that are planted back in April into the specially prepared pits I use for all my brassicas. They do tend to grow tall, and once they are laden with sprouts they have a tendency to fall over, so therefore it is a wise move to stake them with a bamboo cane pushed into the soil near the stem and tie them up with a double loop of soft twine. The stake needs to be in place by early winter.

Only pick firm sprouts that haven't blown (they sort of explode and look like loose rosettes of leaves rather than tight buttons), and always pick starting from the bottom of the stem, snapping the sprouts off. They aren't a trendy vegetable, but nothing beats them on the Christmas table. I grew a variety called Wellington and although the pigeons got to them (my fault for forgetting to put the net back on after weeding – never again) they still produced pretty well. They have a fine flavour and are resistant to mildew.

PARSNIPS

Parsnips kind of passed me by in spring, when I should have been sowing them. This crop stays in the soil for a long time, being sown in March and harvested in December, but the taste is worth the wait. Sadly, it was the taste of other plot holders' roots rather than my own, but next year will be different. (How many times have you heard or even said that?)

Parsnips like it sunny, and need a well-drained, preferably sandy soil. Raised beds or tall containers for me then. The seeds are slow to germinate, but once up and running there are only two problems to watch out for: the first is carrot fly (they love parsnips as an alternative); the second is canker, which is a disease that manifests itself as reddish brown or blackened areas at the tops or shoulders of the roots. Put it down to poor growing conditions and possibly irregular watering. The best way around it is to grow a canker-resistant variety, such as Javelin or Excalibur.

Once the leaves have died off the roots will be ready for harvesting. If you wait for a few hard frosts the starch will have turned to sugar and the roots will be as sweet as a …frosted parsnip.

Love your soil

Every good gardener knows that to grow good plants, especially hungry plants grown for produce like most vegetables, it is necessary to grow in good soil. Ken jokes with me that despite all the work I've put in I should move my plot to get away from my horsetail once and for all, but I know that actually I have some pretty good soil, and have considerably improved it over the year. I'm staying put. Maybe you're lucky enough to inherit good soil on your plot or have done a lot of work to get it into decent shape, but as with all forms of gardening, things never stand still and it's important to keep looking after it to get the best results.

To dig or not to dig?

Digging is one of my favourite jobs in the garden – and wonderful exercise too. There's nothing better than digging so hard on a sunny winter's day that you get down to your T-shirt, and the allotment is the perfect place to do it. In a garden you only really dig large areas of bare soil when preparing for planting, but on an allotment it is part and parcel of the winter season.

A good dig over the vacant beds also gave me the opportunity to get as many weed roots out as possible. I only lifted a fraction of what I had dug up the previous winter, which was extremely encouraging, but I know for sure it'll be a few more years of picking out weeds and digging before I can risk making the same bet as Ken – offering a pound to anyone who can find a weed on his plot.

Winter digging also exposes large clods of my heavy clay to the worst or best of winter frosts, helping to break it up and make it more workable come spring. It also turns up a few unwanted bugs for hungry birds.

But there is a no-dig brigade of gardeners who never dig, and I can fully understand their point of view. In early winter a thick layer of compost is put over the entire plot, which the worms then drag down beneath the soil surface. More compost is added as the growing season goes on and plants use the nutrients, and so on throughout the season. These ever-deepening beds are never walked on, either, to reduce any risk of compaction. Exponents of this no-dig method say that you dig enough of the soil when harvesting, and digging, they claim, can damage the soil structure.

I reckon there is a compromise between dig and no-dig. Lots of compost on top of the soil is great, but I think it is good to then dig it in – help out the worms a bit – and get to know your soil. I agree that you should also not walk on the soil, as this is where the structure gets broken down, especially in heavy clay on a wet day. So my compromise suggestion would be: dig if you like it, but keep off the soil as much as you can.

Council compost and worms

After a long compost drought, the compost deliveries started to appear at regular intervals, thanks to Keith getting on the blower to the council. Our compost is made from a collection of green waste from a few of North London's boroughs, including some of my own kitchen and garden waste from Hackney.

You can't hang around when the council compost turns up as allotmenteers flock from all four corners of the site to snap it up. The forking is great exercise and keeps me warm on a fresh, cold winter's day.

Just from the smell of it, I can tell how beneficial it is for the soil, and the plants. It arrives hot and steaming and needs to be grabbed before it all disappears. Although everyone's really polite and there is plenty to go round, the serious growers don't hang around when it turns up. We all know just how lucky we are to get this delivered for free, and how valuable it is as a soil conditioner. Ask your local council whether you can get some delivered to your allotment, and if not, push and ask why not. Find out what happens to your green waste and where it ends up. Recycling is one of the things that is important to all of us, and compost is the most direct and tangible way of getting back what you put in.

It's inspiring to see some of the older men barrowing all day long, keeping them fit and extremely healthy. One day I saw Vincenzo, a keen grower in his late eighties (in fact, 88 at the last count) barrowing a full load up the hill. He was heading in completely the opposite direction from his own plot. When I asked him where he was going he said he was helping the 'old feller' up the hill, as he couldn't barrow so easily! Apparently this 'old feller' is in his mid-nineties! I put it all down to regular exercise and eating all that healthy veg.

I have been stockpiling a little of the compost in my spare compost bin, but even in the winter I've been putting it directly onto my plot. This is the ideal time of year to chuck it on the soil as a mulch on some of the vacant areas, then let the worms do the important job of mixing it into the soil through the winter. I had bought a bag of earthworms on the internet earlier in the year, which is always a fun exercise. The postman drops them through the letterbox in a breathable bag and there's nothing better than winding Cathy up over breakfast with a bag full of wriggly worms. They really are worth the money, though, as they do a wonderful job on the soil. They bulk up quickly, as they start to reproduce when around 3–6 weeks old, and I now have big fat juicy worms coming up everywhere I dig.

Bad muck

Buying in manure from local stables and farms is a way of life for allotmenteers. There is something bizarrely poetic about how a heap of manure steams on a cold winter day, and you know you are doing good as you spread or dig it in. But not always – last year a storm began to brew over the contamination of manure. Plot holders poisoned their plots; fingers were pointed, and chemicals were temporarily withdrawn from the market.

And it all came down to one chemical called aminopyralid.

It was a new chemical introduced in 2005, a herbicide that was used by farmers to kill off broad-leafed weeds in their fields and paddocks. It did a great job. However, the chemical binds itself tightly to any woody tissue in the plants it has killed and these same plants are then gathered up and fed to cattle or eaten in situ. The resultant manure sometimes contains tiny amounts of the chemical, still bound to smaller pieces of woodier tissue. This is then hauled off to allotment sites where it sits around in heaps until the plot holder decides to dig it in, use it as a mulch or bulk up his or her raised beds with it. The fungi and bacteria in the soil start to break down the woody plant tissue and in the process release the tiny amounts of aminopyralid into the soil. And guess what? It can *still* affect any broad-leafed plant root it comes into contact with.

The first signs of this contamination appeared when potatoes were developing cup-shaped leaves and some even formed fern-like leaves. Tomato plants followed suit. Beans became distorted and then everything bar sweetcorn looked bad. Sometimes whole crops withered and died, but on other occasions the plants grew out of the damage and went on to produce a decent crop. Perhaps this is when a real decision has to be made. Should a crop from a plant that had earlier shown symptoms of contamination be used in the kitchen? All horticultural bodies were involved. The clear message that crops should be safe to be consumed was issued. 'Should be' isn't good enough for me.

The problem stemmed from plant material that was potentially contaminated getting into the supply chain. It states clearly on all literature that this shouldn't happen, but once you have a contaminated plot the main question that everyone wants to know the answer to is how to sort it out. The micro-organisms in the soil break down the chemical quickly, and this activity is further increased as temperatures start to rise. The smaller the pieces of manure are, the quicker this decomposition. So the advice was to dig in the manure but not to plant into it for a couple of months; or heap it up and send it back to the farm or stable.

Thankfully our site wasn't affected, although lots of others were. The one piece of advice I can give to anyone who starts thinking about manure at this time of year, is to check with their supplier. Ask if they, or whoever they get their manure from, use aminopyralid. It may be a withdrawn chemical but there are still a few heaps of manure that contain it all over the country.

TOOLS AND TOOL CARE

Some people go to town when buying tools and use a different one for every job. However, Michael on my site uses his lightweight Azada (see below) for absolutely everything; digging, weeding and harvesting, and is always seen with it over his shoulder and leaning on it, chatting. I bought one and now call it my 'ninja' tool. Couldn't live without it.

There are a few other things in my shed, though, that are essential or just useful to have to hand. My allotment tool kit consists of:

Hoe: There are lots of different-shaped hoes on the market; I use a long-handled, stainless-steel Dutch hoe. It needs to be really sharp to cut weeds with minimum work.

Lightweight Azada: This is a great tool for doing so many jobs. It's a mini mattock and hoe in one. You can get them in a variety of weights and sizes, with the larger ones being ideal for clearing and shaping the plot, and creating soil paths.

Leatherman multi-tool: Cath gave me this a few years ago as a present and I always have it in my pocket at the allotment and use it for everything from cutting string and cable ties, to harvesting produce.

Plastic trays: These are really useful for taking pots of seedlings to and from home and carrying them around the allotment. I also use them to harvest smaller quantities of produce. Over the year I seem to have acquired quite a few, but I always need more!

Spade and fork: Stainless-steel forks and spades with wooden handles are the best as they tend to be lighter, cut through the soil easily and don't hold on to wet clay. They are also simple to keep clean and the handle can be replaced if broken. The blade and neck should ideally be made from the same piece of forged steel. Keep the spade sharp with a sharpening stone and it will considerably reduce the amount of effort you need to expend.

Rake: A soil rake is only used to level, break up and refine soil areas. Mine has quite a wide head to cover the soil quickly, but use one that feels the right weight for you.

Trowel and hand fork: Perfect for hand weeding and planting small plants and bulbs. There's a wide range of shapes and sizes available, so choose ones that you feel comfortable with. I particularly like a sharp, long, thin-bladed hand trowel to dig out deep roots of perennial weeds and for planting small plants and sets.

Watering can: Metal is more durable, but it is heavier than plastic. I have two large plastic ones that I can carry full at the same time to save journeys back and forth from the water butts. A free flowing and easy-to-pour 'rose' is the most important accessory.

Secateurs: There are many different designs and price points for secateurs, including ones for left-handers. The cleanness of the cut is all-important: a clean cut allows the wound to heal over and prevents risk of disease. I prefer to use bypass secateurs, which cut like scissors, rather than the anvil secateurs, which cut down against a flat surface.

Trug or bucket: A really useful piece of kit

From left to right – my trusty tools:
1 Leatherman multi-tool, secateurs, hand fork, hand trowel.
2 Fork, rake, hand fork and trowel, Dutch hoe, Azada, spade.

which can be used for gathering debris, carrying compost, or harvesting.

Wheelbarrow: Absolutely essential for compost barrowing, for moving larger quantities of foliage, or even for transporting crops like potatoes (if you get enough!). I use one with a proper air-filled tyre, as I find the solid tyres difficult to push on uneven ground.

Multi-change kits: If you're starting from scratch and don't have any tools already, you might consider investing in a multi-change kit. Some manufacturers make tool handles which have different 'heads' that you can interchange – such as a hoe, rake and broom. These are a brilliant space-saving idea and are ideal for anyone who has storage problems on site. If you do opt for buying this sort of set, it's important to buy the best quality you can afford because the joints and fixing mechanism will get more wear than a conventional gardening tool.

Cleaning tools: A boring job, but treating gardening tools with a little care means they'll perform better and last longer. I always do this job in winter when I have a little more time on my hands than during the other, hectic seasons. You should check over your tools for any damage that can be repaired, then get down to the actual cleaning. First, clean off any excess soil with a scraper and a wire brush, then use a sharpening stone to sharpen the blades on secateurs, hoes and spades. I use linseed oil on my wooden handles and then some lubricating oil on the metal parts too before hanging them up to store, treated and shiny.

Winter problems

WHITEFLY

The major pest you will come across in winter is brassica whitefly. They lurk on the undersides of your sprouts, cabbage and kale and swarm up when you brush past. If you have a close look at your plants you should be able to see flat, oval, green, scale-like young nymphs on the undersides of leaves. These are the little critters busy sucking the sap from your plants.

Brassica whitefly isn't the same as the whitefly you get in greenhouses or on your tomatoes, so don't worry later in the year about cross infestation. Whitefly are present most of the year and, to be honest, plants can tolerant some infestation. But it's the sooty moulds that grow in the excretions of the pests that can clog up crop production. These moulds also make your sprouts less than attractive. You can try to get rid of them by using sprays, some of which are classed as organic. Whatever you decide to use, remember to add a drop of washing up liquid to the mix, as this helps the spray stick to the waxy leaves.

If spraying isn't your thing, however, you can ensure your plants are in good shape to resist attacks by growing them well. Get the soil right in the first place and strong plants will automatically follow. In addition, pick off any dead leaves as soon as they fade and tidy up around plants, removing any debris. Let a few carrots run to seed, too, as this can attract beneficial wasps into your plot, and even just walking around your plot will disturb the feeding patterns of the whitefly. As a last resort, you can simply wash your harvested crops to get rid of sooty moulds before eating.

---·⊱

I mainly sowed onions and garlic directly into the soil, but I also grew some on in cells in case any didn't come up and to fill in a few gaps once I had cleared out any areas during winter.

PLOT ESSENTIALS – WINTER

If you have one day a week at the plot, make sure you:
- Empty and mix up the compost heaps before refilling the bins.
- Order seeds for next year.
- Dig over vacant soil and add compost or muck.
- Check on stored veg and discard anything that is rotten.

Joe's Veg Heroes
Geoff Hamilton
(15 August 1936–4 August 1996)

Geoff Hamilton is a gardening legend. He was a passionate gardener and garden journalist, and presented *Gardeners' World* for 17 years from his own garden at Barnsdale in Rutland. He was a committed and pioneering advocate of the organic approach, which he helped to demystify and popularise. I spoke to his son Nick, who along with his wife, Sue, is carrying on the organic gardening tradition at Barnsdale.

Geoff Hamilton

Allotment and veg garden Barnsdale, Rutland. The allotment is 888 square metres, the Elizabethan veg garden 121 square metres, the parterre 187 square metres, and the ornamental kitchen garden 216 square metres.

Soil type Heavy clay soil that sits over limestone bedded in with beige clay. At points in the garden the topsoil is only a spit's depth over this layer of limestone.

Biggest growing problem Growing any root crop on the heavy Barnsdale clay. Most years we had carrots and parsnips that, when harvested, would not have looked out of place and Doctor Who, they had so many tentacles. However, being aware of this problem my father started digging organic matter into the allotment area immediately on moving up here and we have spent the last 25 years doing exactly the same. Now we are finally getting single root carrots and parsnips that don't take most of the evening to peel.

Time spent on vegetable growing He was out in the garden as much as he could be.

Favourite tool His wooden-handled, stainless-steel spade and home-made blade cleaner. He loved digging; a gardener's spade is almost like an extra limb.

Favourite crop If pushed it would have to be between sweetcorn, melons and tomatoes. You know even today I still occasionally have a look over my shoulder when picking a melon, just to check my father's not there!

When did Geoff first grow vegetables? He seriously started growing vegetables when he became the editor of *Practical Gardening* magazine. He did so primarily to provide pictures for the magazine as they had no area used by the company for this purpose.

Why did he love growing fruit and vegetables so much? He came across as having a passion for veg because he had a passion for gardening, but of course the great reward of a well-planned, well-kept, productive area was not just the beauty, as you get with ornamental areas, but the fact that ultimately you got to eat it all.

Why did he think 'growing your own' was so important? The benefits to health and well being, with the ultimate joy of being able to pick it fresh and therefore eat vegetables that tasted as they should. He saw the great

enjoyment of gardening as being in the doing, and there could be nothing better than having physical rewards for the physical energies expended.

What did he do with the excess produce? My father hated waste, so if he had an abundance of anything that would not last he would give it away to anybody he knew, and often people he didn't know!

What is the best piece of growing advice you were ever given by Geoff? I suppose it was the advice given to me as a young child when I began with my tiny vegetable plot in the garden. He explained to me that most of the time when the seed doesn't germinate it is not something that I had done wrong and that I should never give up, but try again the next year.

Did Geoff have a mantra? No, not really, apart for his advice about not giving up after one crop failure. Geoff was way ahead of his time as an organic gardener.

Why do you think did he wanted to be organic in the first place? He became aware of the organic movement and would never dismiss anything out of hand until he had investigated it. After looking into it he began his trials at Barnsdale, which lasted approximately three years, after which the garden was run on his organic principles. The reasons for starting the trials in the first place were no different to the ones that turn most gardeners organic – it's healthier for you, your family and the environment.

Afterword

It feels good reflecting over my first year as a fully-fledged allotmenteer. On the whole I see myself as a positive thinking chap, but I am also a no-nonsense pragmatist, and tend to look neither forward or back through rose-tinted spectacles. My time on the plot so far has been tough at times, but it has far exceeded my expectations and overall has been extremely enjoyable, fulfilling and rewarding. I now feel confident growing my own fruit and vegetables and going forward will be more instinctive and decisive about what and how I grow.

Gardening is all about enjoying the simple processes, the physical connection with the soil, being creative and moving forward by learning from your mistakes. That's what makes it so special. I know I garden professionally, but I feel that my plot has helped me in other parts of my life, too. Whatever job you do or life you lead, an allotment and growing your own can only be a positive thing in that it increases your understanding and very enjoyment of food. But it goes beyond the produce, as it will also connect you with like-minded people and a genuine community built on generosity, respect, friendship and knowledge. I also found it was the best stress buster. After an hour or two on the plot any worries and anxieties just float away.

What would I say to someone thinking of taking one on for the first time? I would say 'Go for it'. Do it your own way and get stuck in! Here are a few clichés that may see you through times of trouble: 'You get out of it what you put in'; 'It's a game of two halves Brian'; and in the deeply philosophical, but undeniably true words of my mate Bob, 'It ain't the end of the world 'til it's the end of the world!'.

I'm often asked if I'm keeping the plot on, or was it all just for the TV? Well, I'm not going to set myself up and say I'll be there forever – who knows what'll happen in the future? – but we're certainly keeping it going for the foreseeable future, that's for sure. Whatever does happen though, I do know that somewhere or other I'll be growing fresh fruit and veg for the rest of my life for two reasons: one, I'm hooked; and two, you just can't beat it!

	Soil	Aspect	Row spacing	Plant spacing	Germination	Time to maturity	Sow outside	
BRASSICAS								
Cabbage (*Brassica oleracea Capitata Group*)	rich, well drained, alkaline, compacted	sheltered	40 cm (16 in)	40 cm (16 in)	10 days	20 weeks	April – August	
Calabrese (*Brassica oleracea Italica Group*)	rich, well drained, alkaline, compacted	sheltered	45 cm (18 in)	45 cm (18 in)	10 days	16 weeks	May	
Cauliflower (*Brassica oleracea Botrytis Group*)	rich, well drained, alkaline, compacted	sheltered	45 cm (18 in)	45 cm (18 in)	10 days	16 weeks	April – May	
Kale (*Brassica oleracea Acephala Group*)	rich, compacted	any	45 cm (18 in)	45 cm (18 in)	10 days	20 weeks	April – June	
Kohlrabi (*Brassica oleracea Gongylodes Group*)	alkaline, compacted	any	30 cm (12 in)	30 cm (12 in)	2 weeks	16 weeks	April – July	
Broccoli (*Brassica oleracea Italica Group*)	rich, well drained, alkaline, compacted	sunny and out of strong wind	45 cm (18 in)	45 cm (18 in)	10 days	9 weeks	April – early May	
Brussel Sprouts (*Brassica oleracea Gemmifera Group*)	rich, well drained, alkaline, compacted	sheltered to avoid plants rocking	45 cm (18 in)	45 cm (18 in)	10 days	36 weeks	May	
ROOT VEG								
Beetroot (*Beta vulgaris*)	remove stones and weeds before sowing	any aspect	15 cm (6 in)	10 cm (4 in)	2 weeks	12 weeks	March – September	
Carrots, (*Daucus carota sativus*)	free draining, ideally sandy	sunny for early varieties; slight shade for maincrop	15 cm (6 in)	15 cm (6 in)	2 weeks	10 – 16 weeks	March – August	

Sow under cover	Plant outside	Plant under cover	Harvest	Store	Pests/ diseases	Joe's recommended varieties
March – May	May	n/a	varieties all year	shred, blanch and freeze	whitefly, cabbage white butterfly	Greyhound: early summer lots of heart and few outer (tough) leaves; January King: winter hardy cabbage with purple-tinged leaves; Primo: great summer cabbage with rock hard, ball-shaped heads.
February – May	May	n/a	May – August	freeze after blanching	whitefly, cabbage white butterfly	Olympia: large, tasty heads followed by lots of sideshoots – it wil crop all summer; Samson: vigorous plants that mature quickly; Fiesta: freezes well and a heavy, reliable cropper.
January – March	April	n/a	varieties all year	freeze after blanching	whitefly, cabbage white butterfly	All the Year Round: everyone's favourite as it is reliable and tastes so good; Avalanche: good for growing closely together for smaller heads, or wide apart for beauties; Clapton: resistant to clubroot and produces large white heads.
August – November	May – July	n/a	all year	cut and come again – leave leaves on the plant	whitefly	Black Tuscany: strappy black/green leaves that are tasty and look great; Dwarf Green Curled: great for poor soils and windy sites, and it tastes good.
March – May	n/a	n/a	July – November	freeze after blanching	flea beetle	Blusta: purple bulbs with crisp white flesh that is slow to turn woody; Kolibri: another purple-skinned, white-fleshed root with bitter free taste.
March	May	n/a	December – March	freeze after blanching	cabbage white butterfly, whitefly	Belstar: great taste, good colour and plenty of small heads; Marathon: quick, tasty and plenty to crop; Summer Purple: green stems, purple florets and super tasty.
end of February	June	n/a	November – February	freeze after blanching	cabbage white butterfly, whitefly	Trafalgar: one of the sweetest sprouts around; Brilliant: early sprouts and lots of them; Nelson: sprouts stay on the plants well.
February – May	March – August	n/a	July – November	clamp or sand box	flea beetle	Boltardy: the best for early sowings as it doesn't run to seed easily; Burpees Golden: great looking roots; Cylndra: great for slicing into salads.
February; October for super early or late crops	April	February; October	June – November	blanch and freeze, sand box, clamp	carrot fly	Flyaway: good resistance to carrot fly; Parmex: deliciously sweet, golf ball-sized roots.

	Soil	Aspect	Row spacing	Plant spacing	Germination	Time to maturity	Sow outside
ROOT VEG (CONT.)							
Parsnip (*Pastinaca sativa*)	well drained, ideally sandy	sunny	15 cm (6 in)	30 cm (12 in)	3 weeks	32 weeks	April – May
Potato (*Solanum tuberosum*)	deep, well drained	sunny	30 cm (12 in)	60 cm (24 in)	3 weeks for chitting; shoots emerge 3 weeks after planting	18 weeks	April – May
Radish (*Raphanus sativus*)	fertile soil that doesn't dry out	partial shade prevents plants from running to seed	5 cm (2 in)	5 cm (2 in)	1 week	8 weeks	April – September
Swede (*Brassica napus Napobrassica Group*)	well drained soil that doesn't dry out	full sun	25 cm (10 in)	45 cm (18 in)	10 days	20 weeks	May – June
Sweet Potato (*Ipomoea batatas*)	moist, fertile, well drained	sun, sun, sun	60 cm (24 in)	45 cm (18 in)	slips root within 3 weeks	28 weeks	n/a
Turnip (*Brassica rapa Rapifera Group*)	fertile soil that doesn't dry out	sunny	20 cm (8 in)	20 cm (8 in)	1 week	10 weeks	February – August
LEGUMES							
Broad Bean (*Vicia faba*)	not fussy but organic matter improves the crop	sunny and sheltered	25 cm (10 in)	25 cm (10 in)	10 days	12 weeks	October – April
French Bean (*Phaseolus vulgaris*)	fertile soil that doesn't dry out but doesn't get waterlogged!	sunny, sheltered and warm	20 cm (8 in)	20 cm (8 in)	10 days	12 weeks	May – July
Pea (*Pisum sativum*)	plenty of organic matter prevents drying out – the nemesis of peas	sun is good but slight shade can help in a hot summer	30 cm (12 in)	10 cm (4 in)	10 days	15 weeks	March – July

Sow under cover	Plant outside	Plant under cover	Harvest	Store	Pests/ diseases	Joe's recommended varieties
February – March	n/a	n/a	November – February	sand box or clamp for up to 3 months	canker and carrot root fly	Gladiator: quick to mature and resistant to canker; Javelin: good crop of tasty roots; Avonresistor: a tried and tested variety producing good crops.
chit in March	April – May	n/a	July – September	clamp for 2 months, hessian or paper sacks	blight	Sarpo varities: great croppers and resistant to blight; Charlotte: a waxy salad potato; Swift: first out of the blocks and produces great tasting, bumper crops.
March	n/a	n/a	all year	sow and harvest a few at a time – keep in fridge for a few days	flea beetle	Scarlet Globe: crispy and hot; French Breakfast: one of the most popular varieties and rightly so – easy cropper; Sparkler: very fast and reliable cropper.
n/a	n/a	n/a	September – December	leave in the ground and lift as required	mildew on leaves	Marion: great crops of heavy roots; Ruby: sweet roots.
March	June	start slips in March	October	sand box for 2 months	aphids	T65: good crops of tasty roots; Georgia Jet: heavy crops when watered well – no protection required once frost has finished.
November – December	n/a	n/a	May – December	sand box for 2 months	flea beetle	Atlantic: fast growing and reliable; Golden Ball: this one's really tasty
n/a	March	n/a	May – August	freeze after blanching	blackfly	The Sutton: best for smaller gardens and delicious beans; Aquadulce Claudia: best for sowing in autumn and winter and again, prolific crops; Green Windsor: massive crops of long pods.
April – May	June – July	n/a	August	freeze whole pods; leave beans to mature, shell and store dry	aphids	Cobra: a great climbing French bean that produces hundreds of pods per plant; Blauhilde: stringless, purple pods, tasty; The Prince: excellent for freezing and one of the tastiest beans around.
February	April	n/a	July – September	freeze after blanching	aphids	Hurst Greenshaft: long pods crammed with tasty peas – delicious; Kelvedon Wonder: good all-rounder, resistant to some diseases – tried and tested variety; Feltham First: good crops and great for sowing in autumn.

	Soil	Aspect	Row spacing	Plant spacing	Germination	Time to maturity	Sow outside
LEGUMES (CONT.)							
Runner Bean (*Phaseolus coccineus*)	loads of muck and stuff and they will be happy	warm, sheltered	45 cm (18 in)	15 cm (6 in)	10 days	15 weeks	May – July
ALLIUMS							
Garlic (*Allium sativum*)	fertile, rich soil that drains well but keeps moisture around roots	warm, sheltered	30 cm (12 in)	10 cm (4 in)	growth starts within 2 weeks	20 weeks	n/a
Leek (*Allium porrum*)	heavy soil is good, waterlogging is bad	sunny	15 cm (6 in)	15 cm (6 in)	2 weeks	30 weeks	March – June
Onion (*Allium cepa*)	good drainage	warm, sunny	30 cm (12 in)	10 cm (4 in)	10 days	15 weeks	April – May
Shallot (*Allium cepa*)	good drainage	warm, sunny	30 cm (12 in)	10 cm (4 in)	shoots appear after 2 weeks	15 weeks	n/a
Spring onion (*Allium cepa*)	good drainage	warm, sunny	15 cm (6 in)	4 cm (1.5 in)	1 week	10 weeks	March – August
CUCURBITS							
Courgette and marrow (*Cucurbita pepo*)	moist, fertile with plenty of muck	warm, sunny, sheltered	1.8 m (6 ft)	1.8 m (6 ft)	1 week	15 weeks	May
Cucumber (*Cucumis sativus*)	moist, fertile with plenty of muck	warm, sunny, sheltered	60 cm (24 in)	60 cm (24 in)	1 week	18 weeks	May – June

Sow under cover	Plant outside	Plant under cover	Harvest	Store	Pests/ diseases	Joe's recommended varieties
April – May	May – June	n/a	July – September	freeze after blanching	aphids, frost	Scarlet Empereror: everyone should grow this tried and tested variety – large crops, early, and no-nonsense taste; Enorma: long, straight, smooth, tasty pods; White Swan: stringless, slim pods and good flavour.
n/a	November – February	n/a	July – August	lift, dry and keep in a cool, frost free space	rust	Purple Wight: doesn't store well but gorgeous eaten fresh; Solent Wight: later maturing with fantastic crops – a good storer; Provence Wight: enormous bulbs and sweet tasting.
December – February	April – June	n/a	October – December	leave in the ground and lift as required	rust, leek moth	Musselburgh: an all-time favourite with thick stems and super hardy; Porbella: sturdy, hardy and resistant to rust; Bandit: one of the best for flavour.
December – February	seedlings in April; sets from September to November and in March	n/a	June – August	lift, dry and keep in a cool, frost free space	rust	Turbo: lovely tasting onion from sets; Red Baron: gorgeous red onions that are so sweet; Bedforshire Champion: mild flavour and great, reliable crops.
n/a	March	n/a	July – August	lift, dry and keep in a cool, frost free space	rust	Hative de Niort: one for the shows but great pear-shaped bulbs that are also tasty; Sante: mild flavoured and great crops; Jermor: elongated bulbs make them easy in the kitchen, great taste.
n/a	n/a	n/a	June – September	lift as required, store in fridge for a week	rust	White Lisbon: mild flavour, quick growing and a reliable favourite; Photon: darker leaves, mild flavour and doesn't mind bad weather; Toga: red and juicy.
April – May	June	n/a	July – October	eat as required or store in fridge for a week	mildew	Courgette All Green Bush: lots of (too many!) green fruits; Courgette Parador: yellow fruits throughout summer; Marrow Tiger Cross: stripy, early fruits that store well over winter.
March – May	June	April	August – September	harvest regularly before cues reach maturity; otherwise a week in the fridge	mildew	Long Green Ridge: don't look the best, but so tasty; Boothby's Blonde: what a name – small cues, crisp and tasty; Burpless Tasty Green: great flavour when picked young.

	Soil	Aspect	Row spacing	Plant spacing	Germination	Time to maturity	Sow outside
CUCURBITS (CONT.)							
Pumpkin (*Cucurbita maxima*)	moist, fertile with plenty of muck	warm, sunny, sheltered	1.8 m (6 ft)	1.8 m (6 ft)	1 week	28 weeks	May
LEAVES AND SALAD VEG							
Chard (*Beta vulgaris var. flavescens*)	moist and plenty of muck	open	45 cm (18 in)	45 cm (18 in)	2 weeks	18 weeks	April – June
Chicory and endive (*Cichorium intybus* and *Cichorium endivia*)	lighter soils are best	bit of shade (grow in between other crops)	30 cm (12 in)	25 cm (10 in)	1 week	16 weeks	April – August
Lettuce (*Lactuca sativa*)	soil that doesn't dry out but never becomes waterlogged	full sun	30 cm (12 in)	15 cm (6 in)	1 week	12 weeks	April – August
Rocket (*Eruca sativa*)	moist, fertile soil	sun but will tolerate some partial shade in the height of summer	15 cm (6 in)	15 cm (6 in)	10 days	12 weeks	April – July
Spinach, summer (*Spinacia oleracea*)	anywhere but poor, dry soil	partial shade	30 cm (12 in)	15 cm (6 in)	2 weeks	18 weeks	March – June; September – November
STEM VEG							
Celery	moist, fertile and packed with muck	sun	45 cm (18 in)	30 cm (12 in)	2 weeks	20 weeks	April – May
Florence Fennel (*Foeniculum vilgare var. azoricum*)	moist	sun but a little shade is okay	50 cm (20 in)	30 cm (12 in)	2 weeks	18 weeks	April – May
PERENNIAL VEG							
Asparagus (*Asparagus officinalis*)	well drained soil is essential – add grit	sunny and sheltered	30 cm (12 in)	30 cm (12 in)	crowns start growing 3 weeks after planting	3 years for a good crop!	grow from crowns planted February to April

Sow under cover	Plant outside	Plant under cover	Harvest	Store	Pests/ diseases	Joe's recommended varieties
April	May – June	n/a	September – November	lift, dry and keep in a cool, frost free space	mildew	Atlantic Giant: one of the biggest around and surprisingly tasty; Jack of All Trades: great tasting and manageable-sized fruits; Fester: sweet fleshed fruit on compact vines.
n/a	May – June	n/a	all year	cut as required	bolting in summer – keep moist	Bright Lights: a mix of varieties that look and taste terrific; White Silver: reliable and a good cropper.
n/a	May – June	n/a	July – October	cut as required	botrytis	Palla Rossa: a classic with large hearts and slightly bitter taste; Glory: a frisee type with tasty, highly-divided leaves.
March	April – August	n/a	June – November	cut as required	slugs and snails	Little Gem: you can pack a lot of plants into a small space and each is tasty; Lollo Rossa: frilly, red and flavoursome – cut leaves as you need them; All the Year Round: medium-sized heads of crunchy, old-fashioned-tasting lettuce; Salad Bowl: loose-leafed plant producing hundreds of tasty leaves to pick when you want them.
n/a	May – August	n/a	July – November	cut as required	slugs and snails	Astro: resistant to bolting in summer and produces smooth, tasty leaves; Runway: serrated, peppery-flavoured leaves.
n/a	April	n/a	April – October	cut as required, store in plastic bags in fridge	mildew	Hector: doesn't bolt easily and resistant to mildews – it also produces a great crop of 'baby' leaves; Picasso: hightly textured and superb-tasting leaves.
March	May – June	n/a	August – September	cut as required; one week in the fridge	slugs and snails	Granada: great tasting sticks that last well in the fridge; Victoria: exceptionally crunchy sticks and very tasty; Loretta: smooth sticks, great flavour, self-blanching and easy to grow.
March	May – June	n/a	July – September	lift and use as required	bolting in summer – keep moist	Amigo: fast growing and can be grown close together – tasty and my favourite; Sirio: large white crops, sweet and highly aromatic leaves.
n/a	February – April	n/a	April – May	cut and savour as required	snails, asparagus beetle	Gijnlim: reliable, producing green spears with purple tips – delicious; Connovers Colossal: reliable, mid-green spears with purple tips, great crops after two or three years.

	Soil	Aspect	Row spacing	Plant spacing	Germination	Time to maturity	Sow outside	
PERENNIAL VEG (CONT.)								
Globe artichoke (*Cynara scolymus***)**	plenty of muck	sun, sun, sun	75 cm (30 in)	75 cm (30 in)	1 month	2 years	plant divisions March to May	
Jerusalem artichoke (*Helianthus tuberosus***)**	plenty of muck	sun	60 cm (24 in)	60 cm (24 in)	1 month	28 weeks	plant tubers February to March	
Rhubarb (*Rheum x hybridum***)**	full of muck, fertile and moisture retentive	sun	1 m (3 ft)	1 m (3 ft)	crowns grow in spring	2 years	plant crowns from October to February	
SUMMER FRUITING VEG								
Aubergine (*Solanum melongena***)**	plenty of muck and free draining	sun, sheltered and warm	30 cm (12 in)	30 cm (12 in)	2 weeks	20 weeks	n/a	
Peppers and chillis (*Capsicum annuum***)**	fertile and water retentive	sunny and sheltered	30 cm (12 in)	30 cm (12 in)	2 weeks	16 weeks	n/a	
Sweetcorn (*Zea mays***)**	anything but waterlogged	sunny and sheltered	45 cm (18 in)	45 cm (18 in)	10 days	20 weeks	May	
Tomato (*Lycopersicon esculentum***)**	plenty of muck	sunny and warm	45 cm (18 in)	45 cm (18 in)	10 days	16 weeks	May	
HERBS								
Basil (*Ocimum basilicum***)**	well drained	sunny and sheltered	15 cm (6 in)	15 cm (6 in)	2 weeks	16 weeks	May	
Chervil (*Anthriscus cerefolium***)**	well drained	sunny	15 cm (6 in)	15 cm (6 in)	2 weeks	16 weeks	June	

Sow under cover	Plant outside	Plant under cover	Harvest	Store	Pests/ diseases	Joe's recommended varieties
n/a	March – May; September – October	n/a	June – July	cut as required; one week in the fridge	slugs, snails, blackfly	Green Globe: big green globe heads; Purple Sicilian: small purple heads and very tasty; Romanesco: big purple heads.
n/a	plant tubers from February to March	n/a	October – December	lift as required; clamp; sand box	slugs and snails	Fuseau: less knobbly and therefore easier to peel – nice taste and plenty of them.
n/a	October – March	n/a	May – July	cut as required – make into pies and crumbles and freeze	slugs and snails	Timperley Early; thick sticks and plenty of them – a great variety; Victoria: smaller sticks but juicy; Prince Albert: an early variety and tasty sticks.
March	May – June	May – June	August – September	cut and use as required; fridge for a week.	botrytis, slugs and snails	Moneymaker: a reliable variety, deep purple, almost black fruits; Black Beauty: strong growing plants even outdoors in warm places; Easter Egg: white egg-shaped and sized fruits – tasty.
March	May – June	April – June	July – September	cut as required; pickle or dry	aphids	Heatwave: be warned, it's hot; Gypsy: great for outdoors and fruits have good flavour; Demon Red: another hot one but smaller fruits and great for pots.
April	May – June	n/a	August – October	cut and cook as required	birds	Swift: what else! sweet, medium-sized cobs, grow well throughout the country; Bojangles: extremely sweet cobs; Minipop: bred for smaller minicobs, sweet and crisp when small.
February – April	May – June	March – May	July – September	use, bottle	blight	Outdoor Girl: a classic tomato in taste, shape and colour; Gardener's Delight: smaller fruits and as tasty as you can imagine; Glacier: great for colder areas, producing terrific crops of tasty toms.
April	May – June	n/a	August – October	pick as required	slugs	Sweet Basil: easy to grow and classic flavour; Siam Basil: great for Thai dishes; Cinnamon Basil: mild and slightly tender so grow indoors or outside in warm areas.
n/a	June	n/a	all year	pick as required	none	Chervil is usually sold simply as chervil or as ready grown plants in garden retailers. Be warned – it sets seeds easily.

	Soil	Aspect	Row spacing	Plant spacing	Germination	Time to maturity	Sow outside	
HERBS (CONT.)								
Chives (*Allium schoenoprasum***)**	any	any	10 cm (4 in)	10 cm (4 in)	2 weeks	16 weeks	March – June	
Coriander (*Coriandrum sativum***)**	fertile	sun with shade in summer	10 cm (4 in)	5 cm (2 in)	2 weeks	12 weeks	April	
Dill (*Anethem graveolens***)**	fertile	sun	45 cm (18 in)	30 cm (12 in)	1 week	12 weeks	April	
Lovage (*Levisticum officinale***)**	any	any	30 cm (12 in)	30 cm (12 in)	2 weeks	16 weeks	April	
Mint (*Mentha species***)**	any	anywhere if kept moist	15 cm (6 in)	15 cm (6 in)	2 weeks	20 weeks	April	
Parsley (*Petroselinum crispum***)**	fertile	any	5 cm (2 in)	15 cm (6 in)	1 month	16 weeks	March – June	
Rosemary (*Rosmarinus officinalis***)**	sandy	sunny	60 cm (24 in)	60 cm (24 in)	1 month for cuttings to root	1 year	May	
Sorrel (*Rumex acetosa***)**	fertile	partial shade	15 cm (6 in)	15 cm (6 in)	3 weeks	16 weeks	March – June	
Tarragon (*Artemesia dracunculus***)**	fertile	sun or partial shade	15 cm (6 in)	15 cm (6 in)	2 weeks	12 weeks	March – June	
Thyme (*Thymus species***)**	light	sun, sun, sun	30 cm (12 in)	15 cm (6 in)	2 weeks	16 weeks	March – June	

Sow under cover	Plant outside	Plant under cover	Harvest	Store	Pests/ diseases	Joe's recommended varieties
n/a	May	n/a	July – October	pick as required	rust	One packet will be enough as they are perennial and once you have them they will last for years.
n/a	May	n/a	July – September	pick as required	none	Confetti: fern-like leaves with a sweeter taste than most varieties.
March	May	n/a	July – September	pick as required	none	Bouquet: dwarf form with ferny foliage.
March	May	n/a	July – September	pick as required	none	Just go for plain lovage seeds – you won't be disappointed.
n/a	April – August	n/a	all year	pick as required	rust	So many to choose from: Pennyroyal, Peppermint, Spearmint – taste before buying plants.
February – April	May	n/a	all year	pick as required	none	Moss Curled is a traditional favourite and Plain Leafed is the tastiest.
March	April	take cuttings in spring	all year	pick as required or hang sprigs in cool, dry shed	Rosemary beetle	Miss Jessops Upright and Corsican Blue: great in the kitchen, but can be tender in the north.
February – April	May	n/a	all year	pick as required	slugs and snails	Sorrel seed is readily available.
February – April	May	n/a	all year	pick as required	none	Russian: mild flavour, strong growing.
February – April	May	n/a	all year	pick as required	none	Gold, Scented, Garden: there are lots to choose from – taste and smell before you buy.

Index

Acknowledgements

THANKS TO:

The living legend that is Phil McCann for his support and encouragement throughout the year as well as his editorial input, without which this book would never have happened.

All at BBC books, especially Lorna Russell, Stuart Cooper and Caroline McArthur for their commitment, professionalism and hard work. All at Smith & Gilmour for making allotment gardening look glamorous. Sarah Cuttle for all her wonderful photography and mutual allotment banter.

The BBC film crew: Mark Scott, my TV director (Mr Invisible) for his overall vision and for asking tricky and probing questions like, 'What are you doing today Joe?'; cameraman Gary 'Sharpshot' Hawkey for his patience and creativity whilst avoiding treading on my precious plants during tricky shots; soundmen Simon Edwards, Pete Sainsbury and Gordon Nightingale for not stopping filming for every single plane out of Stansted (just most of them).

All at the site: my fellow plot holders and friends, Ken, Keith, Manuel, Gary, Trevor, Michael, Sabina, Albino, Vincenzo, Tulip and all the others, for their patience and understanding with all the filming.

To the following vegetable growers, allotment holders, and general gardening icons for all their help and encouragement: Cleve (Clifford) West, Carol Klein, Monty Don, Toby Buckland, Peter Whiting, Joy Larkcom, Nick Hamilton and Terry Walton. Warning – I have most of your mobile numbers for when I get stuck at (or completely lose) the plot!

Allotment artist Chris Cyprus for his wonderful painting of the plot for Children in Need (www.allotmentart.com).

Enfield Council.

As ever, to the Thursday night footy boys (Fat Dad's FC). It's no coincidence that 2008 was the year I took on my allotment and also won the much-coveted Player of the Year award!

Sarah Moors, Rosemary Edwards and Nick Patten, and all at Gardeners' World BBC Birmingham for supporting me throughout, but most importantly for just letting me get on with it!

Brenda James who encourages us all and always helps out at the plot, and in memory of Colin James, a huge lover of life who will always be in our hearts.

Special love and thanks to Cathy, Stanley and Connie for all their digging, weeding, harvesting, eating and overall good old Swifty spirit!